ON THE BATTLE LINES

On the Battle Lines

Edited by

MALCOLM BOYD

MOREHOUSE-BARLOW CO.

NEW YORK

Printed in the United States of America

All royalties from the sale of this book

have been assigned to The National Council

of the Protestant Episcopal Church in the U. S. A.

for use in

advance work in race relations.

Contributors

J. C. MICHAEL ALLEN, B.D.

Rector, St. Mark's-in-the-Bouwerie Church, New York, N.Y.

Contributor, *Modern Canterbury Pilgrims*

LEE A. BELFORD, S.T.M., PH.D.

Chairman, Department of Religious Education, New York University, and Associate Minister, Church of the Epiphany, New York, N.Y.

Author, *Introduction to Judaism*

MYRON B. BLOY, JR., M.A., S.T.B.

Episcopal Chaplain, Massachusetts Institute of Technology

MALCOLM BOYD, S.T.M.

Episcopal Chaplain, Wayne State University

Author, *Crisis in Communication, Christ and Celebrity Gods, Focus, If I Go Down to Hell;* Plays: *Boy: An Experience in the Search for Identity, Study in Color* (trilogy), *The Community*

Contributor, *Christianity and the Contemporary Arts*

JAMES P. BREEDEN, B.D.

Canon, St. Paul's Cathedral, Boston, Mass., and Adviser on Civil Rights to the Bishop of Massachusetts

RICHARD E. BYFIELD, B.D.

Rector, All Saints' Church, Palo Alto, Calif.

Co-author, *Your Money and Your Church*

ROBERT W. CASTLE, JR., S.T.B.

Rector, St. John's Church, Jersey City, N.J.

DON H. COPELAND, D.D.

Founder and Director, The World Center for Liturgical Studies, Boca Raton, Fla., and Canon (Liturgiologist), St. Luke's Cathedral, Orlando, Fla.

WALTER D. DENNIS, S.T.B.

Vicar, St. Cyprian's Church, Hampton, Va., and Instructor, American Church History, Hampton Institute

DUNCAN M. GRAY, JR., B.D.

Rector, St. Peter's Church, Oxford, Miss.

JAMES A. GUSWELLER, S.T.B.

Rector, Church of St. Matthew and St. Timothy, New York, N.Y.

MICHAEL P. HAMILTON, B.D.

Episcopal Chaplain to Faculty and Graduate Students, University of Southern California

JAMES G. JONES, B.D.

Formerly Executive Director, St. Leonard's House, Chicago, Ill., and Jail Chaplain, City Missions, Diocese of Chicago; now Executive Secretary, Episcopal Charities, Inc.

CHARLES H. LONG, JR., B.D.

Rector, St. Peter's Church, Glenside, Pa. (Also Instructor in Missions, Philadelphia Divinity School)

PAUL MOORE, JR., S.T.D.

Suffragan Bishop, Diocese of Washington

Author, *The Church Reclaims the City*

Contributor, *Viewpoints*

GRANT A. MORRILL, JR., B.D.

Rector, St. Mark's Church, New Canaan, Conn.

JOHN B. MORRIS, B.D.

Executive Director, Episcopal Society for Cultural and Racial Unity

Editor, *South Carolinians Speak*

C. KILMER MYERS, S.T.D., L.H.D.

Formerly Director, Urban Training Center for Christian Mission, Chicago, Ill.; recently elected Suffragan Bishop of Michigan

Author, *Light the Dark Streets*

SCOTT I. PARADISE, B.D.

Associate Director, Detroit Industrial Mission, Detroit, Mich.

DOM BENEDICT REID, O.S.B.

Superior, St. Gregory's Priory, Three Rivers, Mich.

THOMAS R. THRASHER, B.D.

Rector, Chapel of the Cross, Chapel Hill, N.C.

ARTHUR E. WALMSLEY, S.T.B.

Executive Secretary, Division of Christian Citizenship, National Council, Protestant Episcopal Church

Editor, *The Church in a Society of Abundance*

WILLIAM A. WENDT, S.T.B.

Rector, St. Stephen and the Incarnation Church, Washington, D.C.

GEORGE W. WICKERSHAM, II, B.D.

Minister, Tamworth Associated Churches (including St. Andrew's-in-the-Valley, Tamworth), N.H.

GIBSON WINTER, B.D., PH.D.

Associate Professor, The Divinity School, University of Chicago

Author, *Love and Conflict: New Patterns in Family Life, The Suburban Captivity of the Churches, The New Creation As Metropolis*

WILLIAM A. YON, B.D.

Director of Christian Education, Diocese of Alabama

LAYTON P. ZIMMER, S.T.B.

Rector, Trinity Church, Swarthmore, Pa., and Representative of, and Consultant to, the Bishop of Pennsylvania in Areas of Racial Tension.

Contents

11

Preface

The Gospel relates God to man in a radical way; that is, because of the Gospel, man is radically related to the totality of human life in God's world. This is why Christians in our contemporary society are called to a special involvement in the specific social issues marking today's world.

The contributions in this book are written by men who accept Jesus Christ as Lord of the totality of human life, instead of relegating Him to lordship only over a narrow spectrum of life, labeled "religion." These men are priests and bishops in the Episcopal Church. As a whole, they do not deal in an abstract way with their subjects, but represent a solidarity of involvement in them.

MALCOLM BOYD, EDITOR

PART I

THE JUNGLE OF THE CITY

1. The Technological Complex

SCOTT I. PARADISE

All over the West, the first wave of the industrial revolution crept on, without anyone noticing what was happening. It was, of course—or at least it was destined to become, under our own eyes, and in our own time—by far the biggest transformation in society since the discovery of agriculture. In fact, those two revolutions, the agricultural and the industrial-scientific, are the only qualitative changes in social living that men have ever known. But the traditional culture didn't notice: or when it did notice, didn't like what it saw.[1]

Though scientific technology and mass production methods are essential ingredients in the industrial-scientific revolution, the decisive element in this revolution is the large industrial enterprise within which these two essential ingredients are purposively welded together. Among the various kinds of industrial enterprises the large manufacturing corporations are by far the most important. They tend to occupy the strategic centers of the economy and set the standards which influence the thinking of the whole community.

But they are not the only kind of enterprise, for they share the stage with their brother enterprises, the giant public utilities, and surround themselves with their satellites, the suppliers, the distributers, the advertising agencies, trade unions, service industries, and research institutes. Taken all together these various distributions make up the technological complex which more than anything else determines the nature of modern society.

The biggest of these enterprises are the most important because of the great power they wield. Their power is far greater than their size in proportion to the whole economy would suggest, and their influence extends far beyond their corporation property. Part of their power is economic. When a big company transfers operations to a new city, thousands may become unemployed in the old location. When it builds a plant in the rural South, a whole community springs to life. In the mid-fifties, at the point the nation teetered on the brink of recession or worse, the announcement by Harlow Curtice that General Motors planned a big expansion program averted the slump and the nation sighed with relief. An agreement between big corporations and the union on wage rates sets a pattern for the whole industry and perhaps for the area in which the industry is located as well. If U.S. Steel raises its prices, the chances are that prices will rise throughout the industry.

A second part of the corporations' power is other than economic. Corporations have been known to endow cultural centers, influence legislation, and carry out scientific research. And they do more than these things. They influence the very quality of life and thought of the country at large, penetrating areas of life which are quite remote from the corporation itself. The small, family farm with its traditional way of life is giving way to the agricultural industry. Both our military establishments and our hospitals are being increasingly run on the principles of a well-managed industrial enterprise. Even our universities are so taking the coloration of a big corporation that one observer recently referred to them as "the knowledge industry."

The big corporation has not been with us very long. It is, in fact, the first autonomous local institution that has come into existence in our society in five hundred years.[2] It has brought with it a new age which might be called the age of corporations.

The large corporation has its own characteristics, its own rules, and its own nature, which are important not only for itself but for the whole society as well. One of these characteristics is its complex, symbiotic relationship to its geographical location. It is quite possible that many industries may be located anywhere. No longer must they establish themselves in cities or grubby, industrial milltowns. Instead they frequently settle in suburbs or in the open country. Factory workers are as likely to live in a new subdivision or farm as they are to live in a tenement or slum. It is as likely that they drive many miles to work in their own car as walk or use public transportation.

Wherever it is located, however, the corporation plays an important part in the community. It occupies land and pays property taxes. It employs a work force and gives remuneration in return. It requires managers who also become men of influence, if not leaders in the community. And while it pumps wealth into the whole area, it sometimes pumps grime into the air and pollution into the river. Furthermore, a large corporation or two can give a neighborhood special character. What would Pittsburgh be like without steel or Schenectady without General Electric, for instance? But the intimacy of this relationship between a corporation and its geographical environs does not imply an indissoluble marriage between them.

A double standard is involved here. Whereas the community cannot leave the corporation, the corporation can pull up stakes and cause disaster in the community by moving. For the corporation is a super-geographical entity, often with multi-plant operations in several states, with a continental sales organization, and national and international responsibilities. To do their work, managers sometimes have to fly from city to city each week, move gypsy-like from city to city every couple of years, and make decisions that will affect plants and communities thousands of miles from where they sit. Because, therefore, the corporation has no ultimate stake in its particular geographic location, in a special sense it is in it but not of it.

As mentioned, the corporation is far more than an economic organization. It is a distinct community in its own right as well. It offers its employees a second home, a second citizenship, an-

other world to live in quite separate and different from their
place of residence which may be many miles away. In many cases
their friends, their activities, and their style of life changes mark-
edly as they move from one of these worlds to the other. For
some, their life centers around their residence, and they go to
work to earn money to support it. For others, home is a place
to visit and recuperate between bouts with challenges of work
where the real business of living takes place. But in either case
their lives have been fragmented. They have become schizoid;
like amphibians they live their lives in two separate environ-
ments.

The separation between these work communities and residential communities is aided by the impenetrableness of the corporation. Life within it is sealed off from the outside world almost as if by an iron curtain. Although some plants conduct
plant tours for visitors, an outsider hardly ever can learn to know
intimately the complexities and subtleties of life within that
company. Thousands of people with homes virtually on the door-
step of the large factories live there for years without ever seeing
what goes on inside. The approach to one of these large factories sometimes suggests an international frontier. A high fence
topped with barbed wire is broken by a gate at which uniformed
guards watch from a sentry box. On asking for admittance your
credentials are checked by phone to the employee who has invited you, and you are supplied with a visa and often as not with
a guide.

Once within the factory gates the visitor finds the corporate
community surprisingly self-sufficient. A really big corporation
will have its own power plant, its own restaurants, medical services, educational facilities, fire department, police, and judicial
system. In fact, almost every facility offered the citizens of the
civil community will be duplicated by parallel facilities within
the corporation. So impressed have visitors been by these large,
autonomous, separate, impenetrable communities that some
visitors have referred to them as corporate kingdoms or our new
nations. And one perhaps over-enthusiastic Irishman, after a

stay in America, wrote, "When you study the Ford Motor Company, you have before you a great state, perfect in every particular —the nearest that anything on the face of the earth has got to Utopia." [3]

Impressive though it is that corporations may have their own railroads and their own governmental structures, very much more important is the fact that they create their own atmosphere of thought and feeling, their own climate of opinion, company traditions, and hierarchies of value. To try to describe this atmosphere is a perilous task because the thought within a corporation differs widely from individual to individual, and the atmosphere varies from one plant or office to another. Special circumstances sometimes pose as general rules; masses of conflicting intangibles sometimes deceive the acutest observer.

Nevertheless, in spite of the differences between individuals and between corporations, a general identifiable industrial climate of opinion can be described which only slightly distorts the real atmosphere in most firms. Such an atmosphere has a determining influence on how the bulk of men think and what they find they can believe, not only within the corporation, but also throughout industrial society. For instance, one facet of the industrial mentality is that in industry economics is king. Corporate management often feel they cannot afford to act on the basis of non-economic values. Because the corporation "must" meet competition and make profits to survive, economic considerations must come first. Economics may demand that men be laid off who have no prospect of future work; it may decree that a competitor be crushed; it may advise that a suggestion conceived on moral grounds be defended in terms of the balance sheet, or "good business practice." In some circumstances an incompetent may be kept on the company payroll for a couple of years until retirement. The motivation for this management decision might be explained in terms of keeping up office morale instead of mercy. Or, community service awards for employees are as likely to spring from a public relations instinct as from interest in the employees' service to the community. In industry, then, an ethic is demanded which is quite different from that preached from the pulpit and understood to apply in private life.

A special kind of faith in progress is another facet of the industrial mind-set: a belief that human betterment is primarily advanced by technological innovation. Even the fear of automation of some workers in vulnerable situations does not counterbalance the pride, hope, and awe that most people within industry feel in regard to industrial organization and technological development. American industry is dynamic. New products, new techniques, and new ideas ensure that better ways of living will constantly be found. In an age when other kinds of progress are thrown into question, at least here a kind of progress is clear and measurable.

In many corporations, managers also believe that progress must extend to their own company. Technological advance must be matched by the company's growth and an enlarged share of the market. If such advance does not occur, it is often felt that something is terribly wrong. Likewise, a notion of progress extends into the understanding of the goals of individuals within the corporation. For many managers life takes on meaning by reference to promotions. Only by doing increasingly demanding and responsible jobs can talents be developed and success be achieved. Hope in such advancement often leads to a single-minded devotion to the job. And wage earners who feel they have no hope of promotion also expect progress to reward them in the form of ever improving wages and fringe benefits.

An extremely practical bent of mind is another aspect of the many-splendored mentality fostered by the corporation environment. Men are not there to develop abstract theories or engage in metaphysical speculation. A concrete and immediate job has to be done and duty demands that the man in industry get on with it. The result is that questions of ultimate meaning tend to be excluded from corporate discussions. This does not mean, of course, that in such discussions a philosophy is not implied or that values are not taken seriously. But these concerns are kept under the surface and are not often brought into question and scrutinized in discussion. "Far better to deal effectively with limited down-to-earth problems than wallow inconclusively with larger issues of universal importance," the mood within industrial enterprises seems to say. How much more, then, is a consideration of the transcendent ruled out of corporate discussions. The theological dimension can add nothing of benefit and can only contribute a note of dangerous divisiveness to the life of the enterprise. Many will brag that they have worked for years beside a man and never learned what are his religious views or affiliations. Such men may often be moral men and devout churchmen. They may try to apply the Golden Rule in their work and say that they try to obey the Ten Commandments. But, nevertheless, the climate of thought within corporations generally generates the overwhelming sense that questions of theology, of ultimate meaning or purpose, must be kept apart from industrial operations. In fact, it has not even occurred to very many that the two might be brought together. In any case, in spite of an occasional individual who in his own life has been conscious of God in his industrial work and has seriously and tenaciously wrestled with the meaning of the Christian faith in that context, by and large such concerns seem inappropriate. For most people, God has been ruled out beforehand as irrelevant. Within the context of industry, Christianity as it has been traditionally understood seems meaningless, and God is dead.

These habits of thought just mentioned are a few of the elements that make up the climate of opinion within the institutions of the technological complex. This same climate of opinion increasingly pervades and dominates the whole of our society. This is the missionary challenge to the Church in our day. The Church needs to develop new missionary instruments which can effectively engage the life and thought within these institutions. It also needs radically to reshape its theological tools in order that they may be appropriate to the job.

The priest workers in France were one attempt to face this challenge, and the lay academies and industrial missions elsewhere in Europe are another. But in America the few small and fumbling experiments in this direction only faintly echo the European ventures. For the most part, the Church in this country has been curiously myopic. Like the traditional culture referred to by C. P. Snow, the Church seems not to appreciate the dimensions and implications of the revolution of our time, and what it does understand, it generally does not like. We still send missionaries to the people of the dying pre-industrial cultures overseas, but we have not seen as the primary mission field the strongholds of the new industrial culture emerging in our midst. The issue is no less than the effective survival of Christianity in the world of tomorrow.

NOTES

[1] C. P. Snow, *The Two Cultures and the Scientific Revolution*, Cambridge University Press, 1959, p. 24.
[2] Peter Drucker, *The New Society*, Harper and Row, 1950, p. 9.
[3] Quoted in R. L. Bruckenberger, *Image of America*, The Viking Press, 1959, p. 181.

2. At the Core of the City

C. KILMER MYERS

The Church has abandoned its mission to the core of the great city. To say this is to utter a terrible indictment. The poor have been called the "first children of the Church." And the Church, in its absorption by the affluent society, turns its back upon the physical dilapidation and human demoralization of the center-city.

One does not indulge in exaggerated judgment in declaring that if the Church fails to respond to *this* cry for help, in the end it will be unable to respond to *any* cry for help. The nature of the urgency here implied is related to the eschatological notes of the Gospel of God. Wholesale apostasy is implied. It is not a matter of simple failure in strategy nor of misunderstanding the issues. The rejection of the inner-city is the rejection of the Lord Himself; the Lord *is* the poor in the land.

I

When we talk of the "problem" of the inner-city we really are talking about the Negro "problem." At least the fact of the presence of minorities is fused with the fact of the presence of the inner-city. The Negroes have truly poured into the core of the great city. They have over-crowded the sub-marginal dwellings which always house the inhabitants of the ghetto. The

masses of Negroes are unskilled in work and trade. When automation advances, they are the first to feel its impact. Many of
the families display the weaknesses which are the inheritance of
slavery, legal and *de facto*. The added rigors of urban living often
complete the destructive process. Unemployment soars first and
highest among these human beings caught up in the life of the
ghetto which *is* the core of the city.

In the city of New York almost 100,000 young people between the ages of 16 and 19 have job problems. These youths
are either drop-outs from school or high school graduates. The
vast majority are Negroes. They constitute what Dr. Conant
calls a "built-in time bomb" in our urban society. Many of these
youngsters already are unemployable, possessing no work habits
at all. Depressing numbers have retreated into the use of narcotics or cheap wine. The overtones of the kind of despair into
which many have plunged are contained in the German word,
angst. They see no hope of relief. At the same time, they live
in an affluent society which sets a premium on status and material possessions.

The success of the Black Muslim movement in attracting
thousands of hopeless young people lies in its ability to restore
dignity and worth to the business of living. At the same time its
radical break with white American culture re-focuses the attention of the drifters, even though the new world of Islam is a
phantasy. The churches—even the Negro churches—are not
reaching through to these masses. This especially is true in the
great industrial cities of the North and West of the United
States. The Church is equally unrelated to youthful Negro intellectuals. A growing identification of these with leftist movements from the Caribbean and South America undoubtedly is
to be expected. In our world of fantastically rapid social change,
it may well be too late for the middle-class white church to
enter into significant dialogue with these groups. The middle-
class white churches simply are not geared to the kind of revolutionary movements needed in the struggle for freedom among

minority group peoples. The acculturation of the middle-class church makes this impossible. The role of the churches scarcely is distinguishable from that of the social work agencies which are dedicated to meeting needs, *i.e.*, maintaining the *status quo* in the core of the city.

The inner-city is populated with real people. They experience daily life and react to it just as do those among us who live in the suburbs and towns. The civil rights movement has infused with a new spirit the situation in which they daily live. They are developing an identity as a group. They begin to look upon themselves as a power structure among other power structures. Consider Birmingham, Alabama: we thought we understood the power structures of that industrial community in the South; we discover that we do not. This will be the case in city after city both in the South and in the North. Once a means of protest is discovered, nothing can halt the movement of the people who suffer in the inner-city. The question for all of us is this: what is the relation of the Church to these movements? If the middle-class church cannot relate to the aspirations represented in these movements, what kinds of ministries may be developed which may initiate meaningful dialogue and interaction? How far outside traditional ministries will the established churches be willing to move?

No one really knows the answers to these questions but there are signs that they are being raised in many quarters. The few in our churches who have the courage to face these and related questions recognize the extent of our Protestant failure in the core of the city. Many communions presently are engaged in sweeping re-appraisal of their role in the inner-city. Indeed it has been out of a common confession of failure that the new Urban Training Center for Christian Mission in Chicago was born. This exciting ecumenical venture, using the techniques of planned exposure to the city, radical engagement in its life through personal and group involvement in mission, and unhurried, disciplined theological dialogue on the meaning of ac-

tion and confrontation, is itself a sign of the Spirit's movement
in the Church in this land. The Urban Training Center will
not be another graduate school for parsons. It is not conceived
of as a study center for urban work. Rather, it will be a center
for mission in the city, providing that kind of climate in which
thought and action may achieve relevance through a dynamic
co-mingling of one with the other within the Christian Community. It will seek to develop a style of life for the Christian
in the city. It will attempt to recover that interior discipline for
both clergy and laity without which identification with the city
is impossible.

Relating Church ministries to the movement of life and people in the inner-city implies an involvement in the struggle for
political power. It is this aspect of social change that the Church
is not only the least acquainted with but also the most afraid
of. And yet, if the Church in any of its ministries is to move
away from the helping and conserving role of the social service
agencies, it must prepare to rethink its theology of power. There
is a sense in which Church *qua* Church is the mediator in the
power struggle. But this is theoretical because in practice the
Church always has identified itself with the conservative power
structure in society. The Church, ever concerned with its own
preservation as an institution, seldom is able to adopt postures
outside the immediate struggle for power. Indeed it is impossible
for it to do so as an historical institution. If the Church were
to become a radical institution, its roots in the social organism
would be destroyed. Only the idealists think it is possible for
the Church to become a movement for protest and attack only.
The historical impossibility of this casts serious doubts on the
Church's ability to relate as *corpus* to the struggles of the dispossessed. It gives rise to cynicism over the possibility that significant bridges may be constructed between the Church in its
acculterated manifestation and the Church of the poor (assum-
ing that one exists at all!). A realistic view of the Church must
admit its historical identification with the dominant structures
of power and at the same time see within the historical Church

the possibility of a ministry of protest. The propertied Church of the Middle Ages not only gave birth to Francis of Assisi but also found room for him in its life. He continues to be a symbol of the Gospel call to voluntary poverty.

If it is possible for the Church of Identification to tolerate the Church of Protest then there must be a doctrine of "the Church beyond the Church." This is another way of saying that only a radically Catholic doctrine of the Church, one beyond any that American Protestantism yet has tolerated, will be able to contain both the Church as the historical Body of Christ *and* the Church as the Servant in the world. The alternative is to despair of the Church and to seek personal and social ministries outside its recognizable life. Indeed the weaker the doctrine of the Church the more tempting it becomes to choose action outside the Church as the apex of sensitive vocation rather than choose paralysis within the Church.

It will be objected that even this tentative probing toward a *livable* doctrine of the Church re-introduces the spectre of the invisible Church. Perhaps we are searching at the moment for a *practical* doctrine of the Church. Or is this merely a device which will enable us to remain within the Church? The urbanized Christian will reject both the invisible Church and the trickery of a device. He simply will accept history because he knows that neither he nor the Church may jump out of *given* historical skin. He will love his Mother the Church and regard her as beyond criticism. He will see his Mother, indissolubly united with the glorified Christ, as containing within herself the Conserving Church and the Revolutionary Church. The Christian may serve either of these Churches or (what is more likely) both at the same time. Or he may hate the one and love the other. But never will he cease to be united with the Mother whose *typus* is the Mother of God. It is she who feeds him with the Bread, and she alone. To be "outside the Bread" is to wander hungry in the world. The late William Palmer Ladd used to tell his students, "If you are a Catholic, you can be anything."

II

If holy Mother Church is viewed as the Ark of Salvation, her *essential* ministry must be protected both from the silencing habits of the Conforming Church and the critical habits of the Protesting Church. The sacramental person must be above the battle. It is he who gives communion to both armies, so to speak. This he cannot do unless his function is an agreed one, acceptable to both sides. Surely, on the other hand, a bishop whose table fellowship is with the rich and powerful alone cannot act as *the* sacramental person for the Catholic Church. Because he is so identified with the matter of Church preservation, he cannot help but sit at table with the rich and powerful. His fellowship with the dispossessed becomes an act of charity. He is sent to the core of the city even as the professional social worker is sent. He never is their bishop. If he acquires this kind of an identification, the wealth of the powerful is diverted to other more trustworthy helping institutions. The bishop has one foot in the Conforming Church and the other (sometimes) in the Protesting Church. He ought to have both feet in the Catholic Church.

When the bishop rebukes, it is easier to aim his *ex cathedra* prerogatives at the weak. To rebuke the powerful is dangerous and for very real reasons. Hence the essential minister is caught up perennially on the horns of a moral dilemma and, as a consequence, rarely says anything of honest prophetic value—either for the rich or the poor. Meanwhile the mass movements of protest, now aware of the nature of political power, sweep over the ministry of the Ark of Salvation, which cannot any longer feed the men of these movements with the Bread.

The difficulty becomes more acute in view of the Church's tendency to elevate men to the essential ministry because they have related successfully to the Conforming Church. In America there are few Cardinal Suhards. But if the Church of Protest is to live at all with the essential minister he must *never* be identified with either Church in the world. *This minister must be a holy man and this is all we may say of him.*

Perhaps much that has been said above ought to be viewed as a kind of theological phantasy. Or perhaps a parable, a story. Whatever it is, it is saying that we must think deeply about the nature of ministry as we face the symbol of our spiritual defeat, the core of the city. And in any kind of reassessment we ought to remember that always the city is the see of the essential minister.

III

Friction and even open combat between protestant Churchmen and establishment Churchmen ought not dismay us in this land. In the South, baptized Christians use the techniques of direct non-violent action against baptized Churchmen dedicated to the *status quo* in race relations. By these last I do not mean the lunatic fringe which equates Church and Klan membership one with the other. I mean the honest, solid bishops, clergy and laity, dismayed with this new power of protest, who would remove the sting from the onslaught of the dispossessed by urging obedience to the law and order designed to protect the Establishment. The *real* problem here is concerned with the discovery of ways for some Christians to disentangle themselves from identification with the Conforming Church so that they may honestly sing, "We shall overcome," with the Church of Protest. Linking arms with the latter also presupposes a certain amount of trust on the part of the real protestants.

In the core of every city where social revolution has begun, this problem of identification is central. There are some who believe that the solution lies in the education in depth of the suburban Church people. Teach them that the suburbs are part of the city. Show them that because they make a living in the city they therefore must feel responsible for the city. Help them to learn that there is one Church only and that the missionary frontier of this Church is the great city. Some communions even

offer educational materials in packets in order to convert suburban Christians to mission in the core of the city. Undoubtedly
all methods known to us should be tried. They will succeed in
funneling more funds into the coffers of Church urban departments and God knows they need money. Even the clergy aware
of social revolution in the core will take money no matter where
it comes from. But the essential battle lines still will be drawn.
Better housing, job opportunities for Negroes, decent schools,
livable neighborhoods, and all the rest, will come when the dispossessed corral enough power with which to frighten the Establishment; or when the Establishment is wise enough to see
that its own interests are best served by social and economic
improvement of the lot of the dispossessed. Even this last is a
matter of power and the shifting about of it. We need a theology of power in order to understand a theology of the Church.
If the theologians object on technical grounds to the use of
the word theology in this fashion, then let us use the word
ideology.

IV

When the Church which lives in the core of the city learns
to live its own life in dignity and integrity, the Church which
remains in suburban captivity will understand the Catholic
character of the Ark of Salvation. For this to happen a drastic
recasting of our conceptions of ministry must take place.

The Church in the inner-city must learn not to put its trust
either in property or the highly trained professionalized ministry.
Property and its maintenance are not possible in the inner-city.
It is not financially feasible nor is it theologically desirable. The
professionalized ministry has been brainwashed by the middle-
class oriented theological seminary. Its irrelevance in the inner-
city leads to profound frustration and even despair. On the other
hand, the essential ministry must have some professionalized
representation present in the inner-city Church. Relations with
the Church beyond the Church must be preserved. If decisions,

personal and social, are to be made by militants in the inner-
city, these must be reached in the light of the history and experience of the Church, *i.e.*, in the light of *theology*. Theology
is reflection upon the God-man, man-God experience of the
Church in terms of present life situations. The life of the inner-
city Church must not be vacuous; it must be dynamically related to the whole tradition of the Church through a relationship with the essential ministry.

The prophetic function of the Church in the core of the city
belongs primarily to the laity. The assumption of this ministry
is a recognition that prophecy matures only in the world. The
laity live in the world and understand it in a way in which the
sacramental feeders, the clergy, do not. Under the Old Covenant
the prophets were laymen, not priests. The lay prophet must
first of all love Mother Church with all his heart and mind.
She is the base on which he stands. Her view of life—a view
indeed given to her by her divine Head—permeates his decision-
making processes. While the prophet-layman may criticize her
administration of the life-giving sacraments and sacramentals,
he never criticizes the dominical rites as such. He loves her font
and her table. He listens to the oft repeated story of the Good
News of God. Permeated with the Church-spirit he moves out
into the world, speaking prophetically and making power related decisions.

The main concern of the layman is not the preservation of the
official ministry or the church buildings. The life of the layman
is this: he feeds on the Bread and he lives, en-Christed, in the
world. This is all there is; it is so much.

V

The core of the city changes and finally it passes away. It
belongs to a transitory level of existence as a part of creation.
But within the city and its center lives the Catholic Church.
Sometimes her life is hidden and obscure. At other times her
militancy is observable to all. She hymns the Name of Christ

and, again, she barely whispers His Name. Always she is present
—in the decay and rebirth of cities. She is the soul of all cities.
She is glorious because her glory is Christ's. This glory she may
impart to the earthly cities of men.

3. City of Light and City of Darkness

JAMES A. GUSWELLER

The story of the big American city is actually a "Tale of Two Cities," each a distinct entity. It is at the same time a city of light and a city of darkness, a city of culture and a city of degradation, a city of architectural beauty and a city of dark slums, a city of heroism and a city of crime. Whether the American city will prevail as a city of light or a city of darkness depends greatly upon the strength that the Church can muster for her task. Too often the Church has retreated from the overwhelming tasks presented to her by the urban problem, but this work is the most challenging missionary frontier of American Christianity today.

The American family dream, to live in a small house with a garden and a car in the garage, cannot be realized in the inner-city. Although most Americans do not like living in the city because it is too crowded, a third of the American population will spend a major part of their lives in the inner-city. The great upheavals of our population result in movement to the city, and the city also becomes a haven for the immigrant and the minority groups who are searching for a better way of life.

The Church of Saint Matthew and Saint Timothy on West 84th Street in the City of New York was typical of many inner-city parishes before the most recent upheavals in our population. West 84th Street was a stable block, made up of brownstone houses and railroad apartments. Twenty-five years ago each of these brownstone houses was occupied by a single family, and railroad apartment houses had two families on each floor. The street was a quiet one; children could be seen strolling to Central Park with their nurses. It was a middle class neighborhood, which nurtured flourishing churches and good schools. This parish once had over two thousand members.

Today, West 84th Street is a phenomenon of noisy human existence. The old brownstones and railroad apartment houses are still on the block, but they have been cut up so as to contain many more families. The brownstones, built for one family, now house twelve; the old railroad apartment houses are badly overcrowded, and many families are confined to a single room. In and out of the doors of the old houses run Negro and Puerto Rican children who must vie with automobiles for a place to play. They have beautiful faces, but the older residents don't like them, because there are too many of them. The Church of Saint Matthew and Saint Timothy still stands majestically on the block, but its façade has grown dirty with age, and its former middle-class membership has moved to suburbia, leaving only a few elderly people to maintain continuity with its great past. The church's membership has dropped in the past twenty-five years from two thousand to three hundred members. The neighborhood has become a furnished apartment and furnished room neighborhood. This means that the newest immigrant to New York will move to this area to be housed until he can attain financial stability and look for a nicer home.

The newspapers call the block a "slum," yet the people in these furnished rooms and apartments are forced to pay between twenty and thirty-five dollars a week rent. Landlords can get such high rents because there is a shortage of apartments for Negroes and Puerto Ricans. This is a slum neighborhood because the people have crowded in and the facilities of the buildings have broken down under the strain of too much use and abuse.

In 1956, the Church of Saint Matthew and Saint Timothy undertook a mission to West 84th Street. Most of the parishioners no longer lived anywhere near the neighborhood, but they still felt that a church that does not make its witness within its immediate environs does not really have a right to exist. The parish church is a cell in the body of Christ and as a cell in Christ's body, the parish must minister in His name. It must be a fellowship for Christ; it must proclaim the Gospel to its neighborhood. A church surrounded by so many people certainly must placard Christ before them. Saint Paul said of his mission, "Necessity is laid upon me" (I Cor. 9:16), and this is particularly true of the inner-city church.

In 1956, West 84th Street was a Spanish-speaking block. To adjust to the new population, the parish held Spanish language services and opened a Community Center for the children and adults of the neighborhood. As the church moved closer to the people, many Puerto Rican Christians responded to its ministry and made it their spiritual home. The older congregation supported the mission to the neighborhood, and the parish did everything to serve the people, preach the Gospel, and welcome the newcomer into its fellowship.

Many of the Puerto Ricans came to the church first to receive help with their housing problems, or to ask the clergy to intercede for them with the Department of Welfare. The new congregation presented many problems which the average Episcopal parish has never had to deal with before. Many of the men and women lived together in a common-law relationship, which, in Puerto Rico, was a more stable relationship than it became when it was transferred to New York. To teach the people the meaning of Holy Matrimony, and to train the children in the Church's tradition were no small tasks. As the Puerto Rican congregation increased in size, the marriage problem became pressing.

For example, after one of the parish's excellent choir members entered the Confirmation instruction class, it was discovered that she was living with a man in a common-law relationship. He was the father of only the last of her six children; each of the other children had a different father. No one in the family had ever been in contact with any church before their arrival at West 84th Street. The woman was told that she could not be confirmed while she was living with her paramour, and that she would have to ask him either to leave the home, or to marry her and assume responsibility for all the children. Although the woman had never been married, her irregular life actually precluded a marriage in the church. Much to everyone's surprise, this woman put her paramour out and presented herself for the Confirmation class. A few days later her man arrived, demanding to know why the clergy had told her to put him out. It was explained to him that he would have to be legally married and assume the fatherhood of all her children, if the family were to enter the fellowship of Christ's Church. The man consented to do this, and a marriage was arranged, and held in City Hall. The delighted chorister was reconciled to the fact that she could not be married in the church by comparing herself with Grace Kelly, who was married first in a civil ceremony before going to the church.

Eight years ago the Church School of Saint Matthew and Saint Timothy was ninety per cent Spanish-speaking; today, the Church School is ninety per cent American Negro. West 84th Street is no longer a Spanish-speaking Street. The Puerto Ricans fanned out to many other sections of the city when the families could purchase their own furniture and get more adequate housing. Into the brownstones and railroad apartment houses have moved Negro families, arriving in New York directly from various southern states. People change—they come and go—but the Church's mission remains the same: "to give the light of the knowledge of the glory of God in the face of Jesus Christ" (II Cor. 4:6).

Along with the numerous hardships of slum dwellers everywhere, these people have been exploited by criminal landlords. Most of the children cannot have the normal social experiences which the average American takes for granted. A family of eight, forced to live in a single room, finds it impossible to keep the "apartment" clean. The one-room apartment is usually "furnished" with a bed, a few broken chairs, a double-burner hot plate, and a small refrigerator. No family meals are possible simply because there is no table and the whole family could not sit together in the one room. For many in these immigrant families, meals are eaten whenever hunger and opportunity make them possible. Family members turn up in the room individually and scoop up whatever is on the hot plate. Late at night, the adults occupy the bed and the children, some of whom are teenagers, sleep on the floor. In a Confirmation class considering the "last things," a twelve-year-old boy described his conception of heaven as having his family live in an apartment where he could have his own room.

To operate a normal church program in a furnished apartment area of the city is next to impossible. The parishes are not really parishes in the accepted sense; they are processions of people—people moving in and people moving out.

The parish fights for better housing. It fights against slum landlords, and tries to focus the attention of the city on the problem of the slums by undertaking various crusades to help the human situation.

God's Church must come with Christ's message to people, so her greatest concern must always be "the people." Municipal governments can devise programs of urban renewal, settlement houses can offer things to do, but only the Church is concerned with the total man; that is, his body and soul. In a slum, the people need help with so many ordinary things, and the kind of help that they need cannot be provided in a single interview or visit.

Each day brings its pressing problem. There was the woman who came to the church in tears. She was the mother of two little children, aged three and four. Two years before, her husband left her because he had become a dope addict and could not support, or be involved with his family. The woman tried very hard to work, pay the rent, pay for a nursery for the children, and feed and clothe them. She was unable to meet all of her expenses and so she sought help from the Department of Welfare. She was treated so badly that out of sheer desperation she picked up a man who consented to support her children. After living with this man for six months, she became pregnant, and she used drugs to destroy the embryo. When a second pregnancy occurred, her paramour told her that he would no longer support her. He offered her seventy-five dollars to seek an illegal abortion, or she could accept the consequences of being thrown out in the street with her two children. This woman was in a miserable plight. She could not simply be referred to a social agency. She needed help on the spot. She desperately needed strength and understanding. God's Church must care about people with problems like these.

The Church may do well to think in terms of having a trained social worker serve with the priest in a team ministry to assist these multi-problem families. Perhaps Christian leaders should think in terms of having two or possibly three parishes join forces to employ a trained social worker who can co-operate closely with the clergy in helping the troubled family or individual.

Because of overcrowding and the breakdown of families in the slum area, children find it very difficult to adjust to school. Many of the children who attend the Church of Saint Matthew and Saint Timothy cannot read. In fact, most of the teen-agers are denied the opportunity to enter military service because of their academic failures. Part of the work of the parish Community House is to offer an academic program, so that children who need help with basic school subjects can receive individual attention, so that they can take their rightful places in their public school classrooms. The Community House has a library of several thousand volumes, all of which have been donated by groups from other churches. This library is open every after-

noon and evening, and it offers a place for the child, who comes
from a crowded apartment, to study and do his daily school
work. Next year, the church will establish a nursery school to
give children from overcrowded homes social experiences, which
will enable them to learn to read when they get into the public
school's first grade. In a very real sense, the church becomes a
second home for many of the families in the neighborhood.

The Housing Clinic tries to get apartments in other sections
of the city for the families in overcrowded buildings, but many
of them don't want to leave. One mother with five children,
living in a single room, would rather stay on the block so that
her children can have the opportunities that the Community
House offers, rather than move to the Bronx or to Brooklyn,
where she could have a four-room apartment. The love that people have for one another, the love that makes them want to
participate in the life of the Church, is part of the fellowship
which Christ came to establish, and which His Church must consider of paramount importance.

The Church of Saint Matthew and Saint Timothy has been
blessed with fine facilities. Numerous friends and foundations
helped the parish construct a Community House building, where
the church now operates a daily program for the children and
adults in the neighborhood, and in which it has established a
Boys' Cadet Corps.

The Church's message is vital in the inner-city. Masses of
people are crowded together, and they are selfishly absorbed in
promoting what they consider their own best interests. He who
is the Way, the Truth and the Life offers healing for the ills
of society, but He is ignored. Somehow, the Church must become equal to her task, and placard Jesus before the teeming
masses of people in the inner-city. Twenty-five hundred years
ago, Isaiah prophesied that the Messiah would be "despised and
rejected of men; a man of sorrows, and acquainted with grief:
. . . he was despised, and we esteemed him not" (Isa. 53:3).
Certainly Jesus is condemned when men ignore Him and reject
Him. The cruelty and crime of modern society pierces Him. He

carries His cross in the midst of mankind's misery and yet mankind fails to notice Him. He carries His cross through garbage-littered alleyways of New York's tenements. It is vital for His Church to make the people see their Redeemer.

There is very little love in the slums. People are suspicious of each other's motives. The love of Jesus can bring people together. Our whole American society is guilty of the breakdown of human relations which makes our city slums possible. Discrimination against people based on color and national origin is a crime for which our whole society stands indicted. The love of God must be spilled forth in this society, so that men's hearts may be inspired by the vision of their Saviour.

4. Race in the City

WILLIAM A. WENDT

In one of his widely televised addresses, the late President Kennedy spoke of the "fires of frustration and discord" existing in every city in our land. Such a statement clearly described the "gut" problem of our day and age, which can be properly entitled "race in the city." The whole problem of racism is, of course, an infection in all sections and communities of the United States and, in a truer sense, the problem of the whole world community. The concentration of people in the cities, however, makes it a special problem there and, most important, it is becoming increasingly clear that the core of this malignancy is to be found in our urban centers. If this infection is to be treated at all—if this condition of a general toxemia in the hearts and minds of people everywhere is to be eradicated— all of man's redemptive efforts must be concentrated in our cities, wherein is revealed better than any other place the effects of man's sinfulness as well as his essential goodness. The racial infection in our land must first be treated in the streets, homes, factories, offices, schools, and churches of the urban centers if a national purge is effectively to take place.

The tragedy is that so little real attention is being given to the many problems that fester in our urban centers. The existing multiplicity of panaceas offered by concerned groups and government officials to alleviate the problems of the city are not

45

likely to do more than salve the ulcers of racism which exist
there. Indeed, too often they are at best designed to lavishly
roof a social structure, the walls of which are dangerously crack-
ing and the foundations of which are literally crumbling. Undoubtedly, the best example of this is the oft-times confused and
divided effort of city planners and urban renewal experts to plug
up the dike against the social revolution taking place in all
metropolitan areas. What can be demonstrated again and again
in their "band-aid" type arrangements is the continual failure to
recognize that the chief component of the city is always *people*,
whether they be Negro or white, busy or idle, en masse or a few
at a time. A community can never be, nor will ever be, just
a mass of buildings or a complexity of structures, and no Uto-
pian plan, however bold, can fill the needs of the city unless
people are foremost in mind.

The failure of city renewal experts is, interestingly enough,
also the underlying failure of other groups in the city, and most
especially the Church. All the concerns and plans of denominations, singly or together, be they promoted by bishops, govern-
ing bodies or lay experts, are built on the sands of destruction
unless the Church boldly and prophetically makes people—all
people—its primary concern. Unfortunately, this lack of concern for people on the part of the Church is undoubtedly best
reflected and best underlined in the Negro's image of the Church
which is, to use William Stringfellow's biting words, "imperi-
ous, condescending and unknowing, indifferent and unloving." [1]
The Negro leaders in our cities smile somewhat cynically at the
recent rush of churchmen and clergymen to join the civil rights
cavalcade. The institutional Church certainly is not exempt from
the charge of being, in large part, a "Johnny-come-lately" to the
righteousness of civil rights.

In short, race in the city, the "gut ache" of our whole social
structure, is continually aggravated by the refusal on the part
of all men and all groups to adhere steadfastly to the biblical
truth that the Almighty God was and ever is concerned about
people. The words of the prophet Isaiah are very descriptive in-

deed of the present plight of the masses of people in our cities today, and, in particular, the Negroes who have been largely contained in the ghettos of our metropolitan centers: "This is a people robbed and spoiled, they are all of them snared in holes, and they are hid in prison houses: they are for a prey, and none delivereth; for a spoil, and none saith, Restore" (Isa. 42:22). Such a condition, such a forgetfulness that there are things owed unto God often at variance with those owed unto Caesar, has led us all astray into a desert of misunderstanding and hatred from which we cannot help but reap continuing bitter tares.

Where is the starting point for all groups and people to face up to the vital problem of race in the city? There is no better place to begin than with a general acknowledgment that all are guilty and all share in the bitter damnation of the times, and all must seek a share in a general atonement. Such an atonement can only result through much thought, work, prayer and a kind of humility difficult for white Americans; but unless this humility is sought and received from the God who cares about His creation, we will continue to be like the man into whose house a number of devils entered in place of the one cast out. Certainly a special responsibility in seeking such humility rests on the Church and its members who stand as professors and examples of Christianity; and it lies with the same heaviness upon all men of whatever faith.

Does any enlightened person, does any sensitive Christian need additional detailed description of the items, causes, and ravages of the infection inherent in our race problem in the city? They should be terribly clear to us all. Numerous articles, books, and speeches again and again have described how the evils of status, greed, social immorality, and irresponsible power have been compounded. These evils, bred in an atmosphere of self-righteousness seemingly inherent in our American culture, produce hatred and distress among the peoples in our cities and destroy human dignity, self-respect, and brotherhood. In continuing wantonly to engage in such evils, man, professing Christian or not, loses his identity as a person and is not perceptibly higher than what we term the "lower animals."

The Negro in the city is tired of the injustices which he experiences in his daily life with the white man in our American society. He is tired of the white man's continuing emphasis on property rather than people, which has fettered him to the ghetto life with which every Negro is familiar. The Negro is tired of being a whipping boy of labor and industry, both of which have exploited him and have denied him any economic security. He is tired of the white society which so often compares the Negro to a little child unfit for responsibilities and, even in doing so, finds no meaning at all in the Gospel words, "Suffer little children to come unto me," and "Even as ye do it unto the least of these, ye have done it unto me."

The tragedy of all this, and what is so clearly evident in all aspects of city life, is that the white man no longer finds it possible to have any empathy for the condition of his Negro brother. The callous manner in which the white man has denied his Negro brother a share in the forming of our society makes it impossible for whites to see and know the vital concerns of the Negro in the city. How long can a man be denied a share in determining the course of the society in which he lives and dies, without crying out in pain and frustration? For the Negro there can be no further denial of his role.

The new Negro has emerged in the city as a person who, having lived in an enforced humiliation and shame, has now discovered the heady wine of pride. In turn, he carries with him the value of true humility. The Negro, more than anyone else, has discovered the need and value of such humility and has exercised it magnificently as a savory for the bitter herbs of humiliation.

So we see in the city today a new people, an exciting new people, who want and intend to have some "heaven on earth." Probably the new Negro in the city is best described in the words of Sterling Tucker, Director of the Urban League, Washington, D.C.: "People are sick and tired of being pushed around. Even poor and frightened people are tired of this. They have been investigated by welfare, pushed around by police, turned away from the employers' doors, slept in the cold and damp so much that they are emotionally ready for any cause or movement which would appear to give them a chance to fight back, and fight back they will, and fight back they should. The question is not one of whether there should be a fight; the question is one of whether the fight shall be waged against the problems or against people." [2]

The crucial concern for all of us in dealing with the problem of race in the city is involved in the fact that the Negro in the city has much indeed to forgive. Can the white man accept forgiveness? Were the Negro "Paul Bunyanesque," one could still be justified in saying, "It will take a big man to forgive such treatment." The white man, on the whole, expects his forgiveness for half a loaf or, if several of our Southern Congressmen had their way, none at all. The question that looms largest to the white man in our cities today is how prepared or willing is he to grant the Negro the right to forgive.

It would seem now that most white men in the city may grant the Negro his baker's dozen of civil rights legislation—and it will be years before the courts will have established the precise intent and meaning of the legislation—but can and will he open his arms fully to the complete sharing process demanded by the Negro? Then, too, where can a city find leadership for the whole action of forgiveness which must take place? The white man often points to some Negro spokesman as overzealous or opportunistic, and says that he tends to be concerned more with racial hatred than racial justice. This may be true, but is understandably human in some instances—and Negroes are human, too. Certainly examples of hatred in white society are numerous indeed. Where can we procure medication for this plague of social injustice in our urban centers which has poisoned colored and white, rich and poor, educated and illiterate and, most unhappily, much of our useful leadership? What ought to be the way of atonement on the part of all men?

Here is an enormous opportunity for the leadership of the Church, but it must show a creative, prophetic Christianity. It dare not be a leadership of words; it must be a leadership of action, to the redemption of what many Negroes think of as a "white man's religion." The Negro is truly sensitive to Christianity as a way of life at the moment. Dare the white man, so much longer committed to professed Christianity, fail in equal sensitivity? As things are shaping up, the Church and churchmen of both races may be the only ones committed to exercise love and charity, to be quick to justice and equity. While our hearts and minds silently and sincerely murmur "Amen" to the recognition and realization of these aims, we dare not falter in any action which would express them.

The two races, regardless of the consequences of civil rights legislation, are going to have to live with each other, and only by living in and with love and justice is there really hope for a genuine partnership. That this will require more than ever an exercise of prophetic leadership, there can be no doubt; that it will require for many a re-evaluation of the dynamic of their faith in Christianity cannot be doubted. That leadership and this re-evaluation, both for the individual and the institutional Church, are needed *now*.

This is a creative task for a vital faith. Can Christians measure up to it? Are we fit to lead this atonement in our urban centers and, in turn, our whole society without a weak-kneed surrender to expediency? In simplest terms, are we prepared to be Christians, and, by the exercise of Christian love, exorcise the hate that threatens to destroy our large metropolitan centers?

Are *you* prepared to be a Christian in this matter and to exercise Christian love? For if a chain's strength be only that of its weakest link, then the success or failure of this exercise in creative Christianity may be *you!*

LORD, I AM NOT WORTHY

One summer ago, at the Church of St. Stephen and the Incarnation in Washington, D.C., a young English Priest Ordinand was working with his group of 14 young boys in a room used by a women's prayer group for some 40 years. One of the women arrived at the church and discovered this activity and, with great shock, shouted out, "What are all these 'niggers' doing in this room?" The English lad, who had been in the United States for only a week, expressed his certainty that our Saviour and Lord loved both Negro and white alike. She, in turn, indignantly remarked, "You, young man, are just like everybody else around here. You are always trying to drag Jesus Christ into it."

LORD, I AM NOT WORTHY

Oh Lord, we do not have to drag you into it. You are
in the city, humbly serving all the needs of men—
holding out loving hands to join with ours. Grant us
grace to see you in the lives of all our brothers.
Amen.

LORD, I AM NOT WORTHY

NOTES

[1] From "Race, Religion and Revenge," *Christian Century*, February 14, 1962
[2] Speech by Sterling Tucker as reported in *Washington Afro-American*, May 11, 1963

5. Neighborhoods in Flux

ROBERT W. CASTLE, JR.

Neighborhoods in the cities all across America have been, and are, and will continue to be in a state of flux. The conditions that create this never ending change are all inter-related. You can not write about neighborhoods in flux without writing about people, jobs, schools, race relations, absentee landlords, economics, federal housing, police brutality, corruption, politics, and the Christian Church. A neighborhood in flux in the inner-city is affected by all these conditions. The story of one neighborhood often parallels and repeats itself over and over again in cities across the nation.

One such changing neighborhood in a city of the United States is the Bergen-Lafayette Section of Jersey City, New Jersey.

While standing on the corner of Grand and Fairmount Avenues on a warm summer night, talking to a group of young men, one gets the feeling, the sight, the touch and the smell of hopelessness, and despair, and of fellowship and expectancy. You know the young men you are talking to. You have seen them in their few successes and their many frustrations. You know the neighborhood and its people who have gone to greener pastures and the new families who have crowded in. You know those who have pushed the school enrollment to bursting and half-day sessions. You know the once adequate housing which now stinks and rots away as people sleep in the fear of fire and

52

rats. You know the smell of absentee landlords who feed on the
people with indifference and greedy hands, and their smell is
nauseating. You talk of jobs. There are no jobs. You talk of
school and you know many at school don't really care much
for your friends because they are black, or because they or their
parents speak Spanish. You talk about meeting at the Church
to dance or play basketball, and to pray and receive Communion, and while you talk you hear the screaming sirens of the
police, *the Man* who brings order by way of a stick and "you
black son-of-a-bitch." Children run, and run, and run, and mi-
raculously are missed by this car or that bus. You hear someone
call out your name and the friendliness is good. There is a love
that pervades and prevails within the stink, the hopelessness
and the decay, and you know Christ, and you know and are
known in a neighborhood of the inner-city. It is a neighborhood
in flux, yea, in revolution, for the beat of the tambourines from
the gospel church, or the men and women who move stoically
into the Muslim Temple, speak of another change and another
day.

As one walks up from Grand Street to the hill where the
church is that once ministered to the affluent and the upper
crust, you wonder how it all could have happened. You begin
to think about your neighborhood, its people, and you know
this is no isolated situation. The neighborhood you live in is
also in Chicago, New York, Memphis, St. Louis, Los Angeles,
Philadelphia. That's little consolation. You want to understand,
but more than that you want to do something.

This was a neighborhood which once prided itself for its trim
little houses, fancy brownstones, newly erected apartments, fine
shops, respectable people, the stability of it all. Fifty years ago
the neighborhood was a homogeneous, white, middle-, upper
middle-, and upper-class (sociologically speaking) people. The
people were prosperous and the churches they erected were large
and prosperous. Most of the people who lived here believed that
this inner circle of exclusiveness would never end.

When it began to change with the movement of Italian, Irish,

German, Polish and a few negro families into the neighborhood, the affluent began to move. Most of the old families and their children are gone now. The families of the immigrants are almost gone, too. The neighborhood, through the years of change, has become eighty per cent negro. The few remaining white families speak of moving and following their predecessors out of the city, somewhere.

The mobility of the neighborhood goes on. The affluent whites and, increasingly, the affluent negroes move out of the neighborhood. The trained, the skilled, the educated, those who have had the opportunities reach out again for more opportunity. They go to find a place for their children to grow up free from the streets and their dangers and filth. They have gone for status and a place in the sun. They have gone to avoid and escape the negro and Puerto Rican who have moved into the neighborhood. The exodus—always running, running, running. Soon there will be no place to run because the enormous population growth of this country reaches out in every direction.

While there has been a great movement of people out of neighborhoods in the city, there has also been great migration into the urban areas. From where and whence they come to replace their brothers and sisters who have moved on and out is barely discernible. Yet the number grows and grows. Without announcement, fanfare, or fancy moving van, the families keep coming. Most of the new people in the neighborhoods in such flux in the city are rural white and negro from the Southern states and Puerto Rico. They are usually unskilled, untrained, lacking in formal education—people who wake up with a kick in the mouth every day, so to speak.

The new families have come seeking jobs and a new beginning toward a sense of human dignity and value. They come to the city to find jobs that were there 20, 30, 50 years ago, or a year ago: jobs which are no longer there—places of employment move out, too—or the jobs have been claimed by machines the new people do not understand. Many industries have gone from the inner-city to follow their skilled working force into the suburbs, or to find cheaper labor in more rural states, or to seek a lower tax rate community. The jobs that remain deal mainly with services to meet the needs of the city. These are usually filled, demand a skill, or are menial in nature and low in salary.

The state employment office sends you, the newcomer, out on a job that often lasts only a few weeks. You are always sent, if sent at all, for the least desirable jobs. You know yourself to be the last hired and the first fired. There is little opportunity to get into unions, or into apprentice programs. There is no time to be reschooled. There are children to be fed, rent to pay, clothes to buy. You feel even more hopeless. You can begin to see the hopelessness in your kids. You can see it in the face of your neighbor. You want to work. You want to sweat. You can't even sweat. Soon you may not want to sweat any more. Your children may never want to sweat.

Neighborhoods in flux within cities that are in flux may force you to seek local or federal relief or welfare assistance. Often you are treated as a vulture, an animal of low regard. You are insulted, cursed, condemned, made to feel of no value. What you have found in the city, rather than new life with dignity, is further degradation and injustice.

Neighborhoods in flux, such as the one in the vicinity of St. John's Episcopal Church, grow rapidly in statistics. Its population increases, its birth rate is up, the schools become overcrowded, the high school drop-outs multiply, the unemployed grow in number. In a neighborhood which cries out for more stability, there is less and less.

The homes that once housed single families now house six, seven or eight families. Many of these cold-water flats defy description and claim lives physically in horrible fires and spiritually in decay, hopelessness and indifference. Rooming houses spring up—furnished rooms for those who will not stay long. Rents go up as the fat get fatter off the poor. Housing that crowds eight, twelve, or more into one small apartment is everywhere. There is no place to be alone, no place to read, to study, to sleep, perchance to know that *you* are of value and loved in the plan of God.

The mobility of people within a neighborhood will often cause great flux in a given school. All during the school year large numbers of children are shifted from one school to another by some sudden move. The rent goes up, the landlord doesn't want tenants with children in the apartment anymore, you lose your job, the family needs more space—so you move. Needless to say this is disturbing and upsetting both to child and to the school. Adding this to the conditions of segregated schooling and all its evils which work upon a child, plus overcrowded classes, half-time sessions, and many teachers who wish they taught in some newer school with different children—all these factors do not promise much for any child.

Scattered about in the neighborhood are some of the new garbage heaps of the city (not true, certainly, in all cities); the Federal Government calls them projects, low-cost housing, *gardens*. They are usually segregated, run-down, mountains of depersonalized living with hundreds and thousands of children crowded into small areas, pushing for a place to play and run. They are concrete slabs reaching up into the sky and covering all the ground of poor management and local political bungling —all at the expense of human beings.

The neighborhood becomes a home for the old who do not wish to move. Except for the negro and Puerto Rican families, those between the ages of 25 and 50 are gone. Those who have the advantage of education, job training, money, *etc.*, have taken it all with them away from the neighborhood. They seldom, if ever, look back with any care or concern. They now simply pass by on the other side like the Priest and the Levite, reading the ponderous *Times* and never stopping to bind up the wounds they have helped to inflict.

A portion of the neighborhood which was segregated now becomes integrated. The new negro families watch daily the exodus of the white families, and that which was integrated quickly becomes re-segregated, and the negro ghetto of a city continues its stretching and reaching out in new directions to find decent housing for an ever expanding and exploding population.

Neighborhoods which were once peaceful and quiet take on an atmosphere of expectancy. Children are everywhere to be seen, heard and served: children who wear keys around their necks, announcing to all there is no one home until supper time. Mothers and fathers often both work to eke out an existence. Teen-agers in great numbers are idle most of the day. They have not finished school; there are no jobs and there is no place to go. Many stores are vacant along avenues which were once prime shopping areas. Some are filled by perpetual rummage sales, second hand furniture, and store front churches. The avenue becomes dreary and reflects the economic conditions that are taking place in the changing neighborhood.

The night in the summer signals rebirth and people are out sitting, talking. Children play under the artificial light of the city. The new neighborhood is alive with activity, life, sounds, sights, and smells that remind you that you are a part of the suffering and joy of all mankind. It stinks! But it is good! It is not false. It is real! The victories to be won tomorrow will be real victories wrought out of the city. The defeats, the rejections, the disappointments of tomorrow will be real too. One will not feel any pain from them because one becomes immunized after years of the same sufferings and injustices.

The people of a neighborhood in flux, according to many in authority and part of the power structure, deserve no rights. They are poor, so they deserve no rights. They are unemployed, so they deserve no rights. They are black, so they deserve no rights. They live in decaying housing, so they deserve no rights. They live in a neighborhood of high crime rate, so they deserve no rights. The law hates them because they are a problem. The elected officials despise them because they are a bad image in the fair city. The Church wishes they would go away because they are a stain upon its conscience.

Surrounding this neighborhood are the conditions of moral
and spiritual decay in places of power and local government.
Politicians in many of the cities across the United States have
been interested in the neighborhoods in change only when it
has suited their own selfish ends: the forgotten of the inner-city
are not forgotten at election time. Often, elected officials and
the police who condemn the new families of the inner-city are
the same people who feed off the numbers racket and illegal
gambling and others forms of vice. They allow landlords to get
away literally *with murder*; they condemn discrimination in employment and housing but do nothing to change the condition;
they control local boards of education but segregation continues
in the schools; they scream for legalized gambling while they
line their pockets with the gold of the illegal; they allow neighborhoods to rot, streets to be garbage laden, police to beat the
hell out of the helpless; they help create the neighborhood of
the inner-city with its congestion, wine, dope, unemployment,
police brutality, overcrowded schools, segregation, and uninhabit-
able living.

Through all this live people—people who are a part of the
change, people who make up the neighborhood, people who are
alive, sometimes barely; people, young and old, filled with
dreams, hopes, aspirations; people with all sorts of potential,
energy, and creativity.

In a city like Jersey City there are two great businesses. One
is the business of politics: some good, some not so good, and
some rotten.

The second business is survival—the survival of people—the
battle of people versus the city, the battle against all the forces
of sin, the world, and the devil: the last is either elected or appointed. The business of survival is very real to all people, but
especially to the people of the inner-city.

You want to understand the Church—the big churches, the
established church, the white churches and the black churches.
There are white churches and black churches—white churches

who shudder at the neighborhood in flux and who stand stilted, decaying, trying to survive what to them is a holocaust. Black churches strive to have negro members who are really white middle-class, but they, with their white brothers-in-the-cross-of-blood, shed nary a drop of compassion for the neighborhood.

You look around and you see the former great parishes—a mere shadow upon the ground. You see their unwillingness and indifference to minister to the neighborhood by the countless number of store front churches with do-it-yourself ministers, some good, some charlatan. In the flux of the inner-city far too often the Christian Church stands as an integral part of the political power structure of the community. Or the Church is so busy trying to survive that it has lost all sense of its mission to the world and the neighborhood. Those who have been ordained to the sacred service and ministry of Christ no longer cry out in this wilderness, but have themselves become lost in the wilderness.

When three federal housing projects were built near one status congregation, the leadership of that church refused to go into the new neighborhood, protesting that these were not the kind of people to associate with. Some negro status churches still minister to certain groups of negroes—the educated, the West Indian, the light-skinned, only.

The Christian churches in many neighborhoods of the cities of this land have closed their doors for good. Others conduct German-speaking services in Spanish-speaking neighborhoods, or have finally moved to the suburbs to follow *the buck*, leaving behind them people and neighborhoods who are hungry—literally hungry, and hungry for the word of God. *Like a mighty army moves the church of God* away from the struggle of life that exists in the neighborhood. It is heartening to know that this is less true in very recent years. It is a sign, perhaps.

Our Lord Jesus Christ is in the city. God is working out His will in the city. God's will is good. The city is neighborhood. Neighborhoods in the city are in flux. The will of God for the

neighborhoods of our city is good. The will of God is in the
flux. The Church is in the city. The Church must see Christ
and, seeing Him, show Him forth to the people of the city.

The Church is unable to do this as long as it is afraid and
unwilling to involve itself with the lives of the people in changing neighborhoods. The Church can not remain silent in the
world into which it was born. If the Church is to share in the
birth of God in the world, then it must be born in the world.
The Church must be involved with life, the life that affects
people, the life of business, industry, unions, schools, housing,
jobs, and government. The Church needs to dare to be different.
The Church's role is to rock the boat, make waves, shake up the
fat and content, the *status quo*. We are in a revolution—a great
battle of life and death. It is a battle for freedom and human
dignity, for justice and moral and spiritual strength, and not for
mere respectability.

The Church's birth is a birth as our Lord's, not to be ministered unto but to minister. The Church is servant unto all men.
The Church, fellowship of those who gather, looks not to itself
but to the world, to the neighborhood. The servanthood of the
Church in the struggling neighborhoods of our cities is not to
keep patching up the broken pieces of lives that are caused by
the city itself, but to change the city. The Church will always
and must continue to pick up the pieces it can, but it must not
allow itself to be caught up in paternal, benevolent activities at
the expense of really changing the conditions of the city, of its
neighborhood.

The opportunities of the Church in the neighborhood of the
city are great. When you live in a neighborhood of change in
the inner-city, and I do, you can see them. They frighten you
and excite you simultaneously. It is a good feeling, for real peace
comes in the midst of the battle for truth and righteousness and
God. The men and women and children of the inner-city can
rise up and say with St. Paul, "For I am persuaded, that neither
death, nor life, nor angels, nor principalities, nor powers, nor
things present, nor things to come, Nor height, nor depth, nor

any other creature, shall be able to separate us from the love of God, which is in Christ Jesus our Lord" (Rom. 8:38-39).

O holy city, seen of John, Where Christ, the Lamb, doth reign;
Within whose four-square walls shall come, No night, nor need, nor pain,
And where the tears are wiped from eyes That shall not weep again!

Hark, how from men whose lives are held More cheap than merchandise;
From women struggling sore for bread, From little children's cries,
There swells the sobbing human plaint That bids thy walls arise!

O shame to us who rest content While lust and greed for gain
In street and shop and tenement Wring gold from human pain,
And bitter lips in blind despair Cry, "Christ hath died in vain!"

Give us, O God, the strength to build The city that hath stood
Too long a dream, whose laws are love, Whose ways are brotherhood,
And where the sun that shineth is God's grace for human good.

Already in the mind of God That city riseth fair;
Lo, how its splendor challenges The souls that greatly dare—
Yea, bids us seize the whole of life And build its glory there.

WALTER RUSSELL BOWIE

6. And Suddenly Nothing Happens

PAUL MOORE, JR.

In the trampled dignity of the reception room outside the Mayor's office, several restless do-gooders sat, eyes wandering from the Mayor's great mahogany door, upward to the Victorian ceiling and down again, low voices exchanging wry comments. They were fairly prominent do-gooders in their own leagues: the pastors of two Protestant churches, the Executive Secretary of the uptown Y.M.C.A., a representative of the C.I.O. County Council, the presidents of the local American Jewish Congress and the N.A.A.C.P., a board member from the Y.W.C.A., and one bewildered young businessman who took the Boy Scouts seriously. Their mission had to do with alleged police brutality to juveniles.

They awaited the pleasure of the Mayor and had been awaiting it for half an hour. In and out of the room came petitioners from the humbler peoples, who, one by one, were put in the care of seedy officeholders of one kind or another. This was entertaining for a time, but waiting longer than twenty minutes ruffles the dignity of all but the most subservient.

Finally, who should open the great mahogany door but Monsignor O'Sullivan, Pastor of St. Patrick's Church. He graciously received the surprised delegation, apologized for the Mayor's absence, and offered his own services as chairman of the meeting instead. The grievances were aired, one by one, and the Commissioner of Public Safety defended the police, precinct by precinct. The matter would be discussed with the Mayor, they were assured, and every member of the delegation would be advised of the outcome. Each name and address was written down with great concern. The delegation departed, waited several weeks— and suddenly, nothing happened.

Oh, incidentally, the Protestant ministers, on their way home, had been pleased to see St. Patrick's new playground almost completed. A city truck was pouring the last bit of concrete.

Moral of the story: some churches have access to the political power structure and some don't.

Elsewhere in this book the biblical and theological imperative for the Church's involvement with things social is set forth. Suffice it to say, for the purpose of this chapter, that the collision of the Gospel with urban power structures goes back to the time of Jeremiah, or even to the time of Samson and the Philistines of Gaza, although nowadays we are hardly strong enough to pull down the whole structure on our blind heads!

If this tradition of struggle is to continue and produce an occasional victory for the Lord, one must try to understand the nature of the complex of forces within the community. In the following pages, therefore, I will try to describe the urban power structures; to see the interplay between its forces and the Church; to point up some of the anomalies of the subject; and to suggest some ways of dealing with the reality of power. For without such understanding, great efforts are made in good faith—and suddenly nothing happens.

I suppose one untrained in sociology should not venture into this field, for even among sociologists a variety of opinion exists. The school of thought represented by C. Wright Mills and Floyd Hunter tends to center the locus of decision-making in any given community within a definite and fairly constant group.[1] A more recent view sees decisions made by a shifting constellation of groups. Whatever the experts' degree of emphasis, however, it is clear to all that a person's power does directly affect the influence he can bring to bear upon a community decision, and it is also

clear that several powerful individuals of coinciding interests can
bring their corporate power into action with great effect. Further,
such groupings of power relate to each other, interact, and overlap. This relationship is what is meant by the *power structure*.

Urban power structures are evident within business and industry, politics, cultural institutions, social work, and even religion. Minority groups have their own substructures of influence,
affecting, in turn, majority groups. State and national influence
affect all of these both within their fields and through climate
of opinion, economic and political forces, and the mass media.

First, let us look at politics. In the metropolis, political
leaders, by and large, have less prestige than their opposite numbers in business and industry. This is mainly due to the financial
sacrifice involved in political office, and to the fact that in most
cities in the United States the economic leadership lives in the
suburbs outside the city limits and therefore is ineligible for election. Thus city politicians, because of their lack of stature, tend
to be reactors, not leaders. In certain communities, they are
under the direct influence of the Chamber of Commerce because it controls the newspapers, access to campaign funds, and
therefore, votes. In other cities, labor and/or minority groups
exert the direct pressure of votes. In some places, the Church is
politically involved: the Roman Catholic Church in the North-
east, the Southern Baptists in the South, and I daresay the Episcopal Church can throw its weight around with some effect in
suburban communities. (In other words, the cast of characters
in the anecdote with which this chapter opened could shift their
denominations and act out the same scene in another part of
the country.) The politicians of the city vary their programs according to the pressures, individual and combined, of these
power structures. Nor are these pressures always predictable.
For instance, leaders of labor and minority groups do not always
push very hard for "liberal" measures. Whether they do depends
upon where they receive their power: from their constituents, or
from the favors granted them from members of the majority
group.

The economic power structure and members of "society" naturally exert a conservative influence: taxation favorable to the business interests they represent, a minimum of public welfare, a minimum of government control (local is least offensive, international most offensive), anti-labor legislation, a weak civil rights program, and a doctrinaire free-enterprise philosophy across the board. Within this structure, the power any individual commands depends upon his wealth, the size of the corporation he is part of and his position within it, his place in "society" (old family or new), the degree to which he is considered "sound," and of course his willingness to act and his ability to lead. These men may be formally organized in the Chamber of Commerce (more typical of small cities) or informally associated because of friendship or common business interests.

Here are two examples of Chamber of Commerce influence. In Indiana this last year, the State and the Indianapolis Chamber did an about face in their attitude toward civil rights legislation. Some pondered whether this had to do with the stiffening of the federal government's attitude. In any case, much to the surprise of the Indiana Civil Liberties Union and the N.A.A.C.P., the Civil Rights Bill aroused no opposition in the legislature, despite the fact that two years before a much weaker bill barely squeaked through. A couple of years ago I was leading a Christian Social Relations conference for clergy and laymen in Texas. We had a secret poll to find out who they thought ran the town where they lived. The Chamber of Commerce won an easy victory, with the Southern Baptists second. Some said, "What's the difference!"

There are less obvious but important sources of influence. One would not call the cultural community exactly a power structure, and yet a certain difference of orientation on the national level, as the New Frontier, is not unrelated to cultural matters. Locally, the presence of a university can radically alter the social and hence the political climate.

By the same token, a weak group, like the social workers in a

city, can actually make themselves felt far beyond their numbers
because of their skill and knowledge. They are in constant communication with board members who are often members of the
economic power structure; they have the skill to directly influence
legislation; and they are alert to the time and place of decision-
making.

Interesting variations occur within this over-simplified picture.
The extremely rich families and those who are at the very top
of the social structure tend to be more liberal in certain areas
than those who are socially less secure. Some of the former prefer to stand above the struggle, unless a particular project is of
special interest.

I shall assume, arbitrarily, that the readers of this book are
concerned with the achievement of Christian social justice as it
is generally conceived, and that their interest in the power structure has to do with how an understanding of it can make this
achievement easier. Some of the ends of this social justice would
include: equality of opportunity in education, employment, public accommodation, and housing; honest and enlightened government; adequate health, social, and recreational facilities and
services; good schools on all levels and the availability of a variety
of cultural resources to as many as possible. The bind comes
when the attainment of any of these ends runs contrary to the
special interests of a group which has the power to obstruct it.

When I speak of the *Church* working with or against the
power structure, I am afraid you will have a mental picture of
an enlightened Church struggling against an evil or pagan power
structure—martyrs and Roman Emperors hovering in the background! Of course this is far from the case, because almost all of
the upper reaches of the urban power structures are already active members of *a* church. Do you have a picture, then, of enlightened clergy battling stodgy laymen? This might describe
some aspects of the fray, but you know some laymen are more
enlightened than some of the clergy, hard as it is to admit this!
Well, do you see a vision of Christian liberals with swords drawn
against Christian conservatives? Many mean this, I imagine, but

don't dare say it! If we are to be fair and objective, however, we cannot let this picture stand either.

We *are* speaking of the interaction of the Church and the power structure as entities, even though they overlap in membership and spheres of interest. (The Church's interest as an institution may not always be for the common good either.) Some generalizations may clarify the picture further. First of all, those Christians who believe that their Faith has to do with social issues tend to be more liberal-minded than those who think of the Church as a purely "spiritual" affair. For instance, recently the rector of a Northern parish took part in a Prayer Pilgrimage through Southern and Northern cities, on route to the General Convention of the Episcopal Church. The Mississippi authorities jailed him for breaking a segregation law. On his return home, a study of the parish attitudes was made.[2] Those who supported the rector's action argued their case from the tenets of the Faith. Those who opposed it, argued from a secular line of reasoning. The conservatives in this situation did not bring the Faith to bear upon their social thinking. An exception to this generalization, of course, is the anti-communism, anti-gambling, anti-liquor bias of the fundamentalist sect. Generally speaking, however, those who represent the churches officially or semi-officially in social action are liable to hold a more liberal view than the economic power structure. This is also true, of course, of the official statements of the national bodies of the denominations and of ecumenical organizations like the National Council of Churches. The tension exists, therefore, *within* the Church as well as outside the Church and in the community.

Some of the emotion generated by this tension is tinged with fear and hostility, and the pressure of the power structure upon the Church is great enough to prevent the Church from living up to the principles declared by its hierarchies. Thus the sharpness of the Gospel preached and acted out by a parish usually varies inversely with the percentage of members of the economic power structure within its congregation.[3]

The Gospel has considerable influence upon the individual

and domestic morality of the practicing Churchman, but its influence upon his social thinking is less observable. This accounts for the greater militancy of much of Negro church life where Christian principles coincide with secular advantage to a large extent. This is not to minimize the courage of their leaders or the importance of their witness. The member of the Chamber of Commerce, on the one hand, and the Negro pastor who is president of the local N.A.A.C.P., on the other, both attempt to justify the goals of their part of the power structure. "What is good for business is good for the community." "Equality of opportunity is implicit in the Gospel." The reader may agree with one and disagree with the other, but both are attempts at rationalization, and the point is that men in general form their social views according to their social needs and not according to their religious belief.

Besides the degree of liberalism or conservatism which best approximates the social implementation of the Gospel, there is another controversial area: namely, is Christian social action best carried out by individuals anonymously, by individuals in the name of Christ, by a parish, by a diocese, by a Church Federation, or by an alliance of the Church with secular organizations? In other words, in what way can the will of God for society best be effected in view of our knowledge of the urban power structure?

Let us say you, our reader, see a clear need for a low-cost housing unit in a certain blighted area of your city. You happen to be a top-rung member of the economic power structure; therefore you can explore with little difficulty the economic feasibility of securing such housing by private enterprise, and, if it proves feasible, you can arrange the financing. If you find public funds are necessary, and, because of the pressing need, can overcome your bias against this degree of socialism, you are in a position to persuade your colleagues in the Chamber of Commerce, including realtors, that such a project would not interfere with their interests; that in fact it would be a demonstration of the Chamber's public-mindedness. Having, with luck, persuaded a nucleus of key persons, you and they could then work with the Mayor, the Planning Commission and others to begin the necessary governmental procedures to secure funds.

In such a maneuver, your Christian motivation would not be observed; the Church would not be visibly involved; yet a necessary job would be accomplished. On the other hand, if you had discovered this need through your Social Relations department, or used its good offices or those of the Church Federation in the process, an appropriate mention of the same might have its value as a witness of the Church's concern.

Now, let us say that you, our reader, are a day-laborer and a member of a small parish in the aforementioned blighted area. How would you go about a campaign for housing? You would first ask your rector to organize others in the parish who were concerned. Next you would join forces with as many other groups as possible, like N.A.A.C.P., Jewish groups, other churches, *etc.* Having enlarged your own power base, you could then begin to use the social action techniques of petitions, conversations with local political figures, delegations to the Mayor, picketing a reluctant City Hall and so forth. Through the Church, you might also be able to interest some power structure people. The process is long and difficult no matter where you start, but the point I am making is this: in most urban situations of social action, power, not words or principles, is what counts. Thus each person must understand the power structures of his community and where he stands within it before planning a course of action. The two examples above show the approach from strength and the approach from weakness. Each is effective if pursued with perseverance and skill. However, they are probably mutually exclusive.

One unexpected principle is that in many areas a group which lies outside the power structure but which is deeply dedicated has more chance of achieving its end than a group from within which is concerned but not *dedicated* to the cause.

The successful planning of Christian Social Action is affected not only be relative positions of strength but also by a clearly

defined purpose. Is the purpose witness, evangelism through concern, education by example, deepening of involvement for those
participating, or to attain a specific result of social betterment?
If the purpose is witness, the Church should be involved explicitly. If the purpose is the achievement of a result for which
secular or Jewish cooperation is essential, the Church should not
be mentioned. Picketing is a useful technique, but it alienates
the power structure. Sometimes failure with strong witness is
more useful than hidden success to the long term purpose of a
neighborhood parish. In any case, unclear purpose may jettison
success in any area.

Finally, a word should be said about the education of the in-
fluential members of the community in certain aspects of its life
to which they may not have been exposed. All ways of communication can be employed: preaching and the use of news
releases (effectively done recently by the Rev. C. K. Myers in
his attack on the irresponsibility of Protestant businessmen in
New York), demonstrations of various kinds (services and out-
door processions of witness), conferences and lunches aimed at
community leaders, and the cultivation of friendships with them.
One such friendship is often the key to a whole undertaking. A
sustained effort at communication can change the climate of a
city over a period of time, because in every American city there
is a reservoir of goodwill and a sense of justice waiting to be
tapped.

The danger in knowing the workings of the power structure
lies in misuse. Cynical manipulation, alliance with less than
moral sources of power, or unethical methods can cut the Church
off from the source of ultimate power, God. As long as this is
kept in mind, a Christian should not be afraid of the understanding and use of the power which exists as part of God's
world around him. This knowledge and its skillful use can protect and help God's people and can inspire the proper stewardship of power. It relieves the Church from amateurishness in
social action and from the morale-shattering disappointments

which follow when dedicated persons, full of heart, work long and hard with great enthusiasm—and suddenly, nothing happens.

NOTES

[1] See C. Wright Mills, *The Power Elite*, Oxford University Press, 1956, and Floyd Hunter, *Community Power Structure*, University of North Carolina Press, 1953.

[2] See Ellen Naylor Bouton and Thomas F. Pettigrew, "When a Priest Makes a Prayer Pilgrimage," *The Christian Century*, March 20, 1963.

[3] Thomas F. Pettigrew and Ernest Q. Campbell, *Christians in Racial Crisis*, Public Affairs Press, 1959, p. 75 and *passim*.

7. Suburbia—Conformity or Creative Ministry?

GRANT A. MORRILL

The challenge to the Church to act decisively in Suburbia is to be found in those characteristics of Suburbia which usually escape the popularizers of the current image of Suburbia. Close observation indicates that it is difficult to find a "typical Suburbia," difficult to find a "typical suburbanite." Suburban communities can be so designated by their geographical relationship to urban centers, but there is a wide dissimilarity in economic, educational and social make-up from one such community to another. In addition there is an intriguing variety of people who compose a given suburban area. The attempt to describe a given suburban community, economically, socially or spiritually should confound the perceptive person. The "gray-flannel-suited, materialistic-minded, status-seeking suburbanite" is a superficial description, little more descriptive of Suburbia than it is of any other segment of contemporary society in this country. It is difficult to generalize about the motivations, psychological, social and economic, of the individuals of Suburbia with any degree of certainty. The most accurate generalization that may be made of a given suburban area is that of similarity of income and education, but even this generalization breaks down in most instances.

In addition, Suburbia in this country is in a state of flux as the suburban communities are more and more enveloped within the megalo-metropolitan area. This transition is fast changing many of the basic characteristics of what has been known as Suburbia. Skyways, thru-ways and improved transportation, plus the constant burgeoning of population are fast making it necessary that the suburban community be described as a part of the urban society.

No longer is the suburbanite a person who has spent a number of years in a suburban area, nor is he a person who, by virtue of considerable wealth, escaped the furor of the city jungle with only occasional forays into the battle. He is now a man who has lived most of his life in some Mid-Western state, and who now has business interests in the urban center. He believes his children will have the opportunity for a more healthy physical, cultural, educational, and social experience living in a place other than one surrounded by bricks, concrete and mortar. The social psychologists run the danger of doing a grave injustice to the suburbanite with generalizations as to what he is like. Let us not do the suburbanite the indignity of attributing to him motivations and characteristics that may not be his.

How then may the Church act decisively in Suburbia? What is the challenge offered by Suburbia? The Church must recognize that every sector of society is equally important to Christ and needs the renewal of redemption through Him. The Church must approach the suburbanite as a deeply involved urbanite and recognize that every individual in each sector of society is unique in personality and in the potential of his contribution to the advancement of God's purpose.

Basic to any effective work of the Church, be it in industry, urban centers, or suburbia, must be a clear statement of objective. One such statement might be that our objective is to enable people to be the Church: to experience membership in the body of Christ now: to feed upon that body in order that they may be constantly made and remade His body in the world.

Every experimental effort toward the given objective should be constantly evaluated against a statement of purpose.

The challenge to the Church in Suburbia, then, is to teach meaningful participation in the Liturgy, and this includes a growing awareness of participation in the one ministry of the Church. A dynamic and revolutionary ministry to Suburbia may be summed up in the two words: Liturgy and Ministry.

Meaningful participation in the Liturgy has the potential of enabling persons to live with the frustrations, problems and tensions of life in Suburbia, and creates within Suburbia a redeeming community. Meaningful participation in the Liturgy sends the members of the redeeming community out to undertake their revolutionary task in the world.

How can the Church approach the challenge of work in Suburbia? It may approach its task as dealing with individuals as individuals, attempting to discover their basic needs, drives, motives, problems, and ministering to them. As an example, let us take Mr. X. His personality, motivations and problems may or may not be similar to his neighbor's: may or may not be similar to his counterpart who lives in the city.

Mr. X. moved to an Eastern suburban community two years ago from a relatively small city in Texas. Feeling his children would be unhappy in a city, he chose a suburban area, primarily for that reason. It also seemed to offer the good life in terms of the American heritage of a small democratic community governed by town meetings in which there could be freedom to express oneself. Here, he hoped the individual might have the opportunity to develop himself. His problems began very soon after moving when he discovered that Suburbia was not as much a community as he hoped it might be. He finds a lack of interest in him as a person, and it is difficult to decide who his friends may be. In addition he does not quite know who he is in Suburbia, and other people find it difficult to place him in the social milieu. This was no difficulty in Texas because his father and grandfather both lived there, and there was no question as to his social and economic status. In the separation of his economic life in the city and his social life in the suburbs, he finds difficulty evaluating his place in his new community. In Texas and in the city he is a respected person, in Suburbia it is difficult to arrive at a self-image. He is tempted to settle for sheer popularity, by being an all-round good fellow, a golfer, and the life of the party if he is invited to one. In the city he is a man of authority, with a definite image of himself; in Suburbia he may have three years to find status, and then he will move and have to begin the process all over.

More than this, Mr. X. brought with him to Suburbia at least the normal (and perhaps abnormal) emotional stresses of his own psyche with which he continues to have to deal. He has moved ahead in his business status, but he is not sure how far is Up! How high shall he aim? Will he ever be satisfied on a given economic level? He has a full working day to which he must add considerable time for commuting. He will travel frequently for days at a time. When finally home, he wishes to enjoy himself and relax, join community groups and efforts, and so he often deprives himself of necessary sleep. He has the problem of added chores about that dream house. He undergoes longer than usual periods of time between meals. He may like a cocktail or two, or more, and he still must make friends! Time, time—there's not enough of it. All these demands add to the emotional demands upon him.

Add to these stresses the strain of a bigger job with greater responsibility. Old friends are not quite sure of him now that he's "on his way," and basic in all of this is his search for self-identity. And, his two boys! They seem to enjoy everything, work little, and are generally irresponsible! So he deals with them compulsively.

Mrs. X. wants friends too! She will adjust to her new environment as she finds it. But she too has to search. It is difficult. The most direct route to friends seems to be the road of rather aimless activity, but by it she seems to be most easily accepted. Since distances are too great in Suburbia she must chauffeur her children to Scouts, to play situations, to everything they do. She may spend as much as two hours a day in the car! She cannot get all the help she needs with her housekeeping (and probably couldn't afford it if she could). "All that I am I owe to my cleaning woman," one woman has been heard to say. Nothing ever seems to be complete—and she's not sure that her new friends are really friends.

Mr. X. comes home, tired, poured out, to a wife exhausted by her duties and by her own search for identity. She senses that he tends to come home like a management consultant, and having been forced to play the role of the father in the family, she is tired of having to deal with everything and tends to become shrewish. Moreover, they may have spent a little more than they should have on their home and its furnishings, and therefore, while living in the midst of plenty, they are yet experiencing the financial squeeze. Mrs. X. is wide open to a period of emotional depression during the first year of her life in Suburbia.

Then there are the two boys. They need the image and experience of a father who is strong, interested, and concerned. But they see very little of Mr. X. during the week, and on weekends he needs the relaxation of the golf course (if he has been fortunate enough to be accepted at a club). Mother, knowing she must play her own role, assumes much of the father's role also, and becomes increasingly compulsive in her dealings with them. A degree of hostility begins to bend the relationship between children and parents, and the children begin to show signs of delinquent behavior. Suburbia offers them little leisure time activity but life is rather easy for the boys, and they are increasingly convinced that it is easy to be successful in adulthood. Products of this age, they are reluctant to give full commitment to an undergirding philosophy of life.

But the picture is not all negative. There are many positive aspects to the life of this family in Suburbia. Mr. X. is a man of higher than average ability. He is a leader. He will direct the course of the economy. He is alert, energetic, and he is able to "run with an idea" if he is convinced about it. Mrs. X., with her husband, has set high ideals for marriage and parenthood. She is an attractive person, who can make a good presentation of herself in many different and sometimes difficult situations. Both have sufficient educational background to be able to evaluate and discuss ideas intelligently. Both often sense a need for using their gifts to the advancement of other persons, and the community. They want to understand themselves better, and they would like the assurance of a conviction about the meaning of life. They would like to cut through the sham and irrelevances of existence as they know it to a clear knowledge of ultimate truth. They are not sure where to look, and they are weary with the dry bones which have been offered them in the past. They are a little frightened of this prospect, for it might threaten some of the things they hold dear. The children have great potential by inheritance. Hopefully, they will be pushed through to a good education, or as good as the country offers on the average, and they have the potential of becoming leaders in the future.

This family is the focus of the challenge to the Church in Suburbia. If the Church can deal effectively with the needs of the individuals of this family, the Church can work effectively and victoriously in Suburbia.

It is perhaps easier to diagnose the needs, tensions, and problems of individuals living in Suburbia than it is to prescribe how the Church may deal effectively with them. This is at once the challenge and excitement of this ministry. A creative and revolutionary approach to them is essential.

The necessary prerequisite for such an approach is a renewal of parish life. This involves the transition from what most parishes are today, more or less unrelated individuals who *attend* Church, to congregations who *are* the Church. The characteristic mark of this congregation will be a spirit-filled community which by the depth of concern and full commitment of each for all the others endeavors to live out the demands of Christ in their relationships. In this community there will be a continuing search for those common convictions and common commitments that weld them together and enable them to be the

78 ON THE BATTLE LINES

Church as Christ meant it to be. In this community each individual will be honored and given the freedom and support to begin to become the unique individual of infinite worth God intended him to be. All of this is preparation to meaningful participation in the Liturgy.

This kind of congregation can enter into the Liturgy with meaning, and minister life-giving power to Mr. and Mrs. X. and their children. Here Mr. and Mrs. X. will find assistance in their search for meaning and identity. Here they may discover the meaning of being a "new creation" and experience the witness of the Church as a vital body. This community will find the means of incorporating the family X. upon their arrival in town. They will be received in such a manner that they will know themselves to be needed and important in this portion of God's people. They will be given the assurance of acceptance, and with others they will be encouraged to look objectively and honestly at the life in which they now find themselves involved. They will be supported to deal realistically with the loss of meaning and the depersonalization which has invaded their lives in the modern industrial era. They will know themselves to be the Body of Christ, and they will feed on that Body that they may constantly be remade His Body in the world.

In the experience of the action of the Liturgy, as nowhere else, they will find the answer to their quest for identity and a life-giving solidarity with others in Christ. In learning to bring to the Offertory the totality of the world that is theirs, and in which they live, they will know the celebration of the Liturgy begins not in Church but in the secular world with which they deal each day. They will be strengthened in the knowledge that in the Offertory is the promise of a new life and a new world. For here, in this action, the secular with all its uncleanness, tension, frustration, and separation from God's purpose is being offered back to Him that it may come once more under His dominion, be purified for use in His service. God's creative enterprise can begin again through that which has been offered and brought back into relation with Him.

As the X. family understands and experiences the action of the Liturgy, loneliness will give way to at-one-ment with Christ and through Him with the other members of the Body of Christ; despair will give way to a great hope of being a "new creation" in a recreated world; the quest for identity will find its fulfillment as they begin to know themselves as they have been known in the accepting mind of God.

A further insight the X. family will discover in the Liturgy is that they have a function in the ministry of the Church. The Church is close to heresy in its contemporary relinquishment of the ministry into the hands of the ordained clergy. The early Church understood that as there was one Lord, one faith, one Body of Christ, so also was there also one ministry of the whole Church to the world. This ministry may be described as a service the Church has to discharge to the world. As it was one ministry of the whole Church to the world so also was every member of the Body of Christ expected to participate in that ministry. St. Paul urged that God's people be equipped for work in Christ's service to the building up of the Body of Christ. Meaningful participation in the Liturgy will convey to the X. family that exciting and awesome fact that God intends to use them in His redemptive activity in the lives of other people and in society. Thus when a congregation discovers the depth of its inner life as the Body of Christ in the drama of the Liturgy, the individuals of that congregation find themselves thrust out into the life of the world to make real to the world the unity experienced in Christ.

As the X. family grows in the experience of this activity, two significant insights are given them. First, they find that as they discover their ministry, the life of grace that is theirs, they begin to discover themselves on ever deeper levels. They find that he who loses his life in ministry, finds it; that he who offers himself in Christ's name, finds himself accepted of Him and empowered of Him to begin to be a whole person. Secondly, they discover that the carrying out of the ministry that is theirs challenges the imagination and resources of any individual to the point that he

soon longs for the support, guidance, and resources of the Holy
Spirit community. And so while having found their motivation
in the Liturgy, to it they must return to be built up into the
Body ever more strongly.

A congregation experiencing this bi-polar action can minister
effectively in Suburbia through the one ministry of the whole
Church. There must be many avenues to involvement in these
realities.

Four avenues which seem essential are these: first, the formation within the larger congregation of small groups in which
there can be real meeting, real confrontation, and the supporting
relationship of concerned persons. In this small group the individual may be free to express real concerns and grow to new
insights. Second, involvement of youth and adults in the conference setting where, for an extended time, there is opportunity
to deal with the basic issues of life and faith, to build relationship with Christ and with each other, to experience Christian
community in study, worship, and recreation. One ought to be
able to accomplish something of this in the life of the parish
at home, but the greatest inhibitor to new understanding and
change of attitude and effective involvement is that people are
not given the opportunity to meet together sufficiently frequently
for sufficiently long periods of time to enable them to deal adequately with the most important aspects of their lives, and build
the relationship with others through which this can be done.
Third, study opportunities of all kinds, usually of fairly short
duration, using whatever techniques seem to be most suited to
the subject and make-up of the groups: discussion, lecture, panel,
etc. Fourth, various groups that meet regularly to evaluate, plan,
direct the life of the parish in the areas of youth, social relations,
education for all ages, of both short and continuous duration.

All these efforts will offer the individual an opportunity to
contribute his abilities and insights, find involvement, growth in
understanding, ability to participate in dialogue, and a freedom
to carry out a part of the ministry that is his.

PART II

CONTEMPORARY ISSUES
IN THE CHURCH

8. Involved in Mankind

JOHN B. MORRIS

> No man is an island, entire of itself; every man is a piece of the continent, a part of the main; if a clod be washed away by the sea, Europe is the less, as well as if a promontory were, as well as if a manor of thy friends or of thine own were; any man's death diminishes me, because I am involved in mankind; and therefore never send to know for whom the bell tolls; it tolls for thee.
>
> —JOHN DONNE

Ask not for whom the bell tolls. It tolls for humanity on the brink of a global race war. It tolls for the nearly extinct integrity of the Household of Faith. It is heard in yesterday's bombing in Birmingham, or in today's Sanctus recited in the chapel of a segregated school in Atlanta. It echoes so loudly through each day's accounts of racial incidents that we are immunized to its meaning, and have our second cup of coffee without flinching any more. If it stops ringing, there will be no more coffee and no more bad news. All will be caught up equally in the final blasts and the unnoticed silence. There will be no more segregation in that day, as all flesh beholds the Glory of God rising out of unmourned wastelands.

In place of the tolling bell, the children who have been set apart will with one voice praise the Father in His Holiness. There will be no more cattle prods or segregated altars, for those who divided and their victims will sit down together before a high and lifted up Saviour. Ask not for whom the bell tolls then, unless you can bear this vision of ultimate triumph by Jesus Christ on His terms. If it is too hard, then cry for the beloved country and a disobedient Church. Cry for the lingering hate we share, or for our muteness when no one else could speak. Perhaps the tears will keep the bell tolling and put off the time when there is no one to hear. But, if not, there is someone who will wipe them away.

I am persuaded that the issue of race is one of life or death for mankind, and is a matter of survival for the Church. I am persuaded that the bell is tolling its last warning for us *now*. As always, our God is at work in history and will ultimately rule, but His victory may not be pleasing to us who participate in its advent. If the history of the last half of this century is written, I am sure that race will be the dominant factor in its account of the movements of men and nations. Within it all He moves. Of this I am sure.

I am also certain that man's sin is very operative now, both through little men and in the principalities and powers of life, and that race is the chief context for the struggle. It is not that integration is a panacea for the conflict at its deeper level, or that its attainment is Gospel, but simply that the ancient problems of man seem most visibly represented today in things racial. Perhaps another dimension will evolve several generations hence. I think not. I see no basis for confidence based on some theory of persistent and inevitable sin. The racial conflict amongst men and nations seems to move almost inexorably toward some end. The broad sweep of present history as regards race appears as both depressing and perplexing, notwithstanding localized gains and successes. One looks for immediate and primary responsibilities to comprehend. For me, it is the hope that at least the Spouse and Body of Christ, the Church, might be found more faithful when and if the bell stops tolling. I believe, too, that if there are any solutions to the world's ills, perhaps their discovery awaits our greater obedience within the Household of Faith.

What I want to say further about Race, the Church and the

World must be said partly through symbols and pictures, and partly through conceptions of the truth as I understand it. Because you, the reader, are likely a Christian, I shall ask that you come with me into the Church to view and hear these things before the altar where we are accustomed to meeting in the Eucharist. What I say and what you will think will constitute a part of the offering we will make of ourselves. Sit nearby, then, and behold the altar, the cross upon it, and the rich tones of blue and red coming in from the windows behind. Consider how most representations of the Last Supper also have windows behind Our Lord and the Twelve, through which one sees the world. The following is what I see and imperfectly understand as I look out.

Dream and Dilemma, Irony or Hope. I see two continents, an ocean and years apart. One is America in its primeval state of virgin forests when only the Indian inhabited its vastness. Here was the untried crucible for the grand experiment that would determine whether man in all of his diversity of color, language, customs, and religion could live together harmoniously. Perhaps it was a dream that no one had—that the people of the world, breaking out of their original geographical confinement, might come together and live in peace. If God set nations of men apart in creation, or permitted their evolution as racial and ethnic entities, He also put into their hearts the will to quest and discover one another. There is no inherent virtue in sameness.

The stately forest symbolizes the opportunity of the land which was big enough for all, but for the flaws that began to emerge. If there was a moment when the dream was viable, it was short-lived. The symbols of America must include the dispossessed first inhabitant, ships of human cargo, and the cattle prod. Huddled masses did come, but laws decreed their origins. The dream became a dilemma because the New World was never really new. The new land inherited and contributed to the deep thread of racism pervading Western culture, and, indeed, has spawned its most brutal expressions. At our best we have held out the opportunity to be melted and molded, giving up particularity, where physically possible, in exchange for hesitant acceptance.

The other continent which I see was once called dark. It is Africa. In the imaginary picture before me, it alone has partially survived a great war between China and the West. Those African states not themselves annihilated by fall-out have formed a central government, to which South Africa was joined, following its revolution.

After the last explosions were heard, mercy teams set out for the now quiet regions of Asia, Europe and the Americas in search of survivors, but never returned. Perhaps it was the example of the heroism of those black and white Christians that steered the Central Government through succeeding years when some tried to deport all whites to the still radioactive wastelands. Black supremacy still flourishes in some sections of the country, but it no longer has any official sanction, and anti-Christian sentiment is also subsiding. The remnant continent, in this picture of things to come, is now making plans for further expeditions that will determine if human life survived anywhere and decide the advisability of repopulation moves. The Church in Africa is training priests who will go along as chaplains and remain as missionaries if other people are found. On such irony hangs hope for the spread of the Gospel and the reconstitution of civilization outside of Africa. If you have been able to visualize this allegory with me, you will want to turn away, and I am more than ready.

God, the Father. How marvelous is the handiwork of God in all of creation! See how He has created man with both a rich variety of characteristics, and yet a common humanity that must somehow reflect His own breadth and constancy. There is no man to whom I am not a brother, however much I might deny it, for He is our Father. If we assign orders of creation to that which God has made and sustained, we blaspheme Him and seek to revoke His creative action. To deny another is to deny Him and ourselves. That some of my brothers have darker colored skin pigmentation than others is of no more consequence than the fact that some are taller than I am, and some have hair of a different color than mine. It resides within the mystery of creation and evolution, which are both in the hand of God, that different people in various parts of the world display varied superficial characteristics. If it be because of differing environmental conditions, then God be praised for His all-encompassing concern. If there is no pragmatic reason for such differences, and even so, let us thank Him for this canvas of humanity He has painted with many brushes. Let us praise Him for our mobility whereby we can know, enjoy, and love all sorts and conditions of men who are all more alike than different.

How terrible it is for any one to feel or be made to feel that he had better never been born black or white or yellow. Calling none superior, we will exalt blackness and whiteness, and every shade, and yet so ignore them all that color-blindness will mark our relations. If self-consciousness predominates for a while after we have thrown off former ways, through Him we will recover some degree of innocence. But we will remember that the fruit of the tree, which gives us the freedom to love, will also be present to enable us to hate and divide and destroy that which God has created.

God the Son. The most profound thing the Christian can say about race relations is that Jesus Christ died to save all men. Philosophical affirmations about the brotherhood of man are supremely certified in the Cross and Resurrection. In Creation we were marked for adoption, but it is through the Good News of Incarnation and Atonement that our blackness and whiteness are equally authenticated, and the sonship of every man validated. But let Paul say it: "There is neither Jew nor Greek, there is neither slave nor free, there is neither male nor female; for you are all one in Christ Jesus." Marks of caste and class are of no account before the leveling love of God in Christ Jesus. He who was made man caught up all men and lifted us heavenward. Though He probably was of brown skin color, in a poetic sense He was of every color. What blasphemy it is when some dispensers of hate claim "Jesus was a white man," but how true when his universality is portrayed in pictures that symbolically identify Him with His faithful people, whether Oriental, African or Western.

How sad it is that in our proclamations and witness for unity among men of all races we so seldom refer to Jesus who is the unique source of our unity. Watered-down statements about brotherhood, true as they are, pale beside the Gospel's demands which leave no options regarding our kinship with all men. We should not "be ashamed to confess the faith of Christ crucified," nor hesitate "to fight under his banner" against the sin of racial discrimination. What power for social change there would be if more sermons were preached on the Gospel and Race than on the minimal demands of Law and Order or Brotherhood. How much more would people, already prepared and raised in a Biblical tradition, respond to a message about the gentle militancy of Jesus than to such concepts as *satyagraha* and the like. But the end and purpose of it all must be Jesus Christ, for His own sake and not as a means to other goals, important as they may be. Ultimately, in words from the Episcopal Society for Cultural and Racial Unity's Statement of Purpose, we seek "that condition of harmony among people which is the benefit of a mutual recognition of the Lordship of Jesus Christ, so that brothers may dwell together in unity and see Him so lifted up that He will draw all men unto Him."

Christians must join with others of diverse creeds, or none at all, in common cause for civil rights and justice, but when these battles seem over, our task is just beginning. Our unique mission is that we are baptized into the fellowship that believes that "God was in Christ reconciling the world to Himself."

Pentecost and Congeniality. As the Celebration of the Holy Communion at the altar before us draws near, look once again with me at two more scenes that I see traced by the lead and glass by which our vigil here in the Church is illumined. I see two distinct and tragically separated groups of men. One is the Vestry of the parish in its regular monthly meeting. The Church is in a changing neighborhood, but the Vestrymen look considerably more prosperous than the surrounding area. That most live some distance from the Church is indicated by their cars which have attracted the attention of some children who were playing in the parking area when they arrived.

As he walked into the room where the other Vestrymen had gathered, the Junior Warden noted that he'd seen two Negro kids in the group outside, and suggested that they should consider placing a cyclone-type fence around the parking area to prevent possible vandalism. The Rector observed that it would be inconvenient to have a gate locked all week because of the various meetings when the parking space was needed. Another Vestryman agreed it was a poor idea because, as he said, "Those hillbillies will just climb over anyway." He then reminisced about how the neighborhood used to have some of the town's finest families. Most had moved to the suburbs now to get away from the poorer whites who had moved into the large houses converted to apartments. But it was time for the meeting to begin, and he withheld further comment.

The business at hand was typical. The Treasurer reported that the endowment had produced a surplus and that two requests for aid had been received from outside the parish, including one from a nearby Community Service Center which wanted to build a gymnasium. However, the bishop had asked for financial assistance in buying some land in one of the suburban areas, and the funds were quickly expended for this purpose. The Senior Warden quipped that his weekly squash game at the club with the bishop would be even more rigorous if they didn't come through. The Rector expressed mild concern that the new mission might take some of their members, since most of them lived in its vicinity, but someone else told him not to worry because the endowment could carry them for years even if everyone left. The others chuckled, except for the newest member of the Vestry who was also Chairman of the Hospitality Committee. He began, "I think Jim's got a point. The part of town from which our kind of people come. . . ," but he was interrupted when the Junior Warden slammed a window shut as the neighborhood youngsters began bouncing a basketball in the parking area.

There was more of the same, but let us turn aside to the other scene where a group of men is gathered. It is the Day of Pentecost, when the disciples "were all together with one accord in one place." As if by a mighty wind and through tongues of fire, they were filled with the Holy Ghost so completely that even language was no barrier as they spoke of Jesus Christ to those assembled in Jerusalem that day. Persons from all parts of the empire, without regard to national background, language, or color, responded to Peter's call to repentance and baptism, and the Church had several thousand added to its original handful. Indeed, that day it became the Church.

The Lord had not left the disciples without the means to be His witnesses. To their faithfulness was added His Spirit which would strengthen and guide them in their mission as the Church. No divisions emasculated their witness as they appeared before the people "with one accord in one place." Thus launched, the spirit-filled fellowship immediately devoted itself to its work as Church, "to the apostles' teaching and fellowship, to the breaking of bread and the prayers." Nowhere are we told that they were an interracial group. The concept of racial differences meant little to them anyway, and certainly it was of no consequence to them in Christ, whose Lordship overrode all differences. But not since has there been such racial and cultural unity as on the day of Pentecost, when the Church was made strong in its original wholeness and harmony.

The Vestry meeting appears so unrelated to this beginning that it is a relief from contrast when the scenes merge once again into the altar windows. Soon the Eucharist will begin.

God the Holy Spirit and His Church. The primary question for the Church is not about race, but about the nature of the Church. Of course, it is important what we do about the race problem in all of its ugly manifestations, but of more profound significance is the fact that our integrity is on trial in what we are within the life of the Church, the Body of Christ. Indeed, our faithfulness is called into question by everything that betrays our being as Church and stamps us with the characteristics of a club. The latter is selective in spirit or fact. The Church is inclusive, save for its expectation of repentance and baptism. The problem for the Church is not race, but simply that it be itself.

Perhaps it started with Constantine's recognition of the Church, and ever since, we have coveted prestige and privilege and respectability in the community. At its heart the flaw is tied to our response to Christ. Most Christians really do not want a Saviour or feel the need for Him. They were brought into the Church on other pretenses, or they knew it was good for business or necessary for social standing. Inevitably, then, we make the requirement for acceptable group life in the Church one of congeniality. If we can be with our kind of people, and feel a little glow in the process, it helps to tide us over. Even amongst many sincerely committed Churchmen, I fear, there is a feeling that the work of the Church is being done most supremely when a sense of coziness pervades the group. It is easier to be congenial with others when they are like you in terms of social, educational, and financial factors, not to speak of race, which projects the greatest possible gulf in our culture.

Coupled with this enthronement of fellowship in human terms is a massive desire to avoid controversy in the Church; controversy might disrupt the comfortable feeling and cause some people to leave. We seek to create and maintain the life of the Church as if it were a dinner party, or cocktails on the terrace. But the spirit-filled fellowship of Pentecost was not created by a spirit of sociability. If we would recapture anything from that occasion, we must redefine our common usage and meaning of fellowship. How marvelous it is, and yet how ordinary it should be, when we visit a parish and both see and sense a dynamic harmony of persons of diverse racial, social, and economic backgrounds. The rarity of this is a judgment on the nature of our obedience to Christ and our lack of reliance on His Spirit to do what He promised.

While the issue for the Church is bigger than race, I am persuaded that what the Church does about the integration of its own life, and the life of the surrounding community constitutes the most pressing question for Christians today. Rather than seeing it as a problem, I believe we must acknowledge that God is reaching out to us in history and providing still another opportunity for the renewal of His Church. Perhaps our moment for decision has passed, but, even so, we must persist in obedience, and hope that there is time during which we might yet be found more faithful.

The bell cannot be heard now, but, if you have followed me, reader, through these thoughts and pictures, you will know that it is still tolling, and for whom. If you would share the burden of these reflections with me, however, there is yet something else which you must perceive for yourself. There is an opportunity now, for the Eucharist is to begin. The Church has filled, the choir has processed, and all is in readiness. It is well that we have this time together to offer our understanding and fears, our involvement in remedy and our failure to act, for it is from here that forgiveness and illumination can flow.

The Celebrant begins, "Almighty God, unto whom all hearts are open, . . ." and our attention is drawn from the things we have seen and heard to the altar, where we have known refreshment many times before. Soon manifold burdens are again lifted from us, and we join in affirming that it is "meet and right" that we should "give thanks unto our Lord God," and solemnly recite, "Holy, Holy, Holy. . . ." As I open my eyes, I see what I hope you behold also. There around the altar stand a multitude of persons out of every nation and race. The assortment of colors blends with the red and blue tones from the windows above and is beautiful beyond all measure. They appear as a rainbow around the Heavenly Throne. Some are richly attired in flowing robes, while others wear only overalls. Every tongue of man blends harmoniously in praise of God. There are the rich and the poor, the little-known and the well-known, all with outstretched hands, waiting to receive the Body and Blood of

Christ. The priest extends the paten, and we go forward and kneel in the midst of the children of God to be fed.

So it is in every Eucharist that we are united with all men, however far they may seem or whatever the barriers. Between the truth of this reality and the reality of things seen lies the mystery and tragedy of life, but thanks be to God who giveth us the victory in Christ Jesus.

9. Jet-Propelled Gradualism

THOMAS R. THRASHER

"The problem," said General MacArthur, in another connection many years ago, "is basically, theological." No truer, or more important thing can be said about the struggle of the Negro for recognition of his rights in our society. I have never been able to think of the Christian doctrine of God, or of man, in other than personal terms. What follows, therefore, can only be a personal witness, a personal reaction, if you will, to events which have taken place before my eyes, to events in which I have been deeply involved.

I was born of Southern parents in the deep South state of Mississippi. I grew up and was educated in the border state of Tennessee. My residence in the latter years of this process was in Mobile, Alabama. The prejudices native to these regions, the fears, the guilts, the paradoxical attitudes, were my prejudices, my fears, my guilt, my attitudes. When I said, "I love the Negra in his place," I thought I knew what was meant by love, and I thought I knew what was the Negro's place. We were taught to be scornful of common white and yankee who did not know how to treat the Negro. Without being told we seemed to know that no Negro was ever addressed as "Mr.," or "Mrs." If younger, he was John and she was Mandy; if older, they were always "Uncle Tom," or "Aunt Sallie."

Our family, though seldom well off, seemed always to have

94

some Negro help—the washerwoman who always took the clothes on Monday and brought them back on Saturday, the practical nurse who came in to help when babies were born, the old family retainers who could be called on in an emergency, and who called on us in their emergencies, the occupants of the shanties in our neighborhoods where, as small children, we were always welcome to visit and smell the interesting smells of Octagon Soap, wood-smoke, snuff, and Negro sweat.

I seem to remember in the 'teens and in the twenties a constant in our conversation. Wherever conversation started, it always ended with some talk about the Negro problem. We had one neighbor who maintained against us all that the Negro had no soul, that he was merely the highest of the lower animals.

Another neighbor somewhat later had a book which advanced the shocking thought that the race problem could be solved by race mixing. Intermarriage, he suggested, would bring into being a race with the finest qualities of both in the ascendant. Of course we knew, even as small children, about the prominent white men who had colored offspring. But not the wildest radical of our time and generation would have suggested that their mother should have been given a ring or the children a name. The *coup de grace* administered regularly to anyone who suggested a change in our racial mores was the question, "Would you want your daughter or your sister to marry a Negra?"

In ways I cannot now remember I learned to be kind to the Negro, to be firm with him, and never to forget that I was superior. Within the conventions just described, relationship was possible. It was casual, not complete; it was easy, not profound; it was insouciant, never intimate; it was concerned with what mattered, but didn't matter very much. Because words passed between us, we assumed we knew each other. Because, for his survival, the Negro had learned to intuit what the white person desired, was able and willing to hear, and to say it to him, we whites were sincerely convinced that the Negro liked our way of life as much as we did. Thus there grew up between what the Negro called "the decent white man," and what the white called "the good Negra," a *modus vivendi,* mutually satisfactory, axio-matic, permanent. Whenever it was called in question, all we had to do for reassurance was to talk it over with the cook or the yardman. To this day, in spite of all the evidence to the contrary, multitudes of Southern whites continue to hold these illusions as the self-evident truths on which the southern way of life is founded.

The impenetrable barrier against the truth was first breached for me by Winifred Kirkland, who taught me not only the full humanity of the Negro, but also the risks essential to preaching the gospel to every creature. Richard Wright, many years later, slammed me in the face with the knowledge that a Negro could come to maturity in our region without coming into contact with a "decent white man." It was later still that I began to see that decency, like patriotism, is not enough. For decency was a placebo for the sickness of our Southern society, a surface salve for the suppurating sore of white supremacy. We took care of the "good Negras" who appertained to us, who made our lives easy and our way of life graceful, just as in another sense, we stood by and allowed white hoodlums to "take care" of the Negroes who didn't know, or who refused to accept "their place."

Richard Wright, with no tug at his forelock, with no scraping of his feet, looked me straight in the eye and talked to me rudely and passionately about what it meant to be a Negro in a white man's world. Thus I began agonizingly to put myself in the Negro's place, to see why a man might walk up twenty stories to avoid riding in a Jim Crow elevator, to feel in my bowels what any man must feel confronted with daily, hourly, con-stantly appearing reminders that the culture to which he be-longed, the civilization of which he was a part, the society he helped build, was conferring upon him a less than human status.

For a time I lived in Indianapolis, a Mid-Western city with a Southern exposure. I lived there over four years. I was homesick. Only an expatriate Southerner can appreciate how deep a sick-ness this can be. I missed climate, cordiality, and colored people.

But I was deeply shocked when I got back home. I began to see and hear what I had never really seen and heard before. I saw unbelievably decrepit houses inhabited by human beings. I heard the word "nigger" used not as a mispronunciation, but as opprobrium. I cringed at public dinners served by Negro waiters, where "humorous" speakers told stories in dialect which ridiculed the Negro, robbed him of his dignity, and characterized him as stupid, ignorant, criminal, immoral.

At the same time it was my good fortune to be involved in the Southern Regional Council, and through it to begin conversation with Negroes who had attained distinction in our community. I must honestly say that here, and in the years since, I have not been able fully to throw off a consciousness of difference which has impaired a fulness and freedom of discourse between me and those Negroes whom I am grateful to be able to call my friends. I am not certain whether this consciousness of difference is a vestigial remnant of a prejudice consciously disavowed, but subconsciously operative within me, or whether it is a response on my part to the Negro's repressed hostility toward me on account of my "whiteness" and on account of the guilt he sees in me. It may well be a combination of both. Whatever its cause, it is a significant factor in race relations, North and South, East and West. In spite of it, however, real communication has gone on, and the agony that comes from its lack of fulness and freedom may be a kind of non-verbal communication fully as important as the words and the ideas we manage to exchange.

Fully as painful is the complete breakdown of communications with many members of my own race. I can recall a pleasant evening with close friends, the delights of which came to a sudden and complete end when I made the mild suggestion that we should make concessions to the aspirations of our Negro citizens before the minimal rights of our Negro citizens should be crammed down our throats. Then one dear old lady in anger used against me in her own living room what was to her the worst possible epithet, "nigger lover," and I, reacting to her anger, and

missing the real meaning of the term, had not presence of mind
or emotion sufficient to say, "Thank you." Another dear friend
whose person I love, but whose opinions I cannot digest, was
convinced I was a communist. When her investigations turned
up no party affiliations, she let it be known that I was a dupe of
the communists. "What you say about the niggers," said a second
friend, "is totally opposite to what my mother taught me. And
my mother was a saint." I was thus maneuvered into the position of accusing a saint of holding wrong opinions, of speaking disrespectfully about one of whom every Southerner knows
he must speak with utmost reverence, the Southern mother.

I was warned by a parishioner against speaking of the race
problem in the pulpit, because, he said, by continuing to do so
I would alienate a congregation who found me acceptable in
other ways. He, himself, found me "untrue to my Southern
heritage."

I have gone into detail concerning my personal history, my
inner and outer conflicts, because they give some insight into
what appears to outsiders as the irrationality, the senselessness,
of Southern intransigence in the face of inevitable social change.
The mass of Southern whites confront the mass of Southern
Negroes across a wasteland where true encounter is all but impossible. We have gone to different schools; we have attended
different churches; we have different sets of heroes; as Sydney
Smith said of two old ladies quarreling over the back fence, we
argue from "different premises"; in very truth, we speak a different language. That is, we did so, until the day before yesterday.

Then, to the utter consternation of most of us, the sit-ins, the
kneel-ins, the marches began to demonstrate to us that the
Negro was asking nothing less than total equality, equal opportunity, equal access to everything our society offers its citizens. We found him no longer willing to wait while the process
of evolution enabled the white to accept the next small step
the Negro might take on the road to his manifest destiny.

Just as I admire the heroism of those who have risked all, the discipline of those who have endured insult and physical violence, for the sake of their rights, so do I marvel at the speed with which change has been effected. And I do not for one moment deny that much still remains to be done. However, the good strategist consolidates his gains before moving on to his next objective. I hold no brief for the white who sees these gains as calamity. However, by living with these gains for a while, by having the opportunity to see the Negro in his full dignity and magnanimity, he may be enabled to see the demands of the future less as a threat and more as a promise.

I make this suggestion out of twin concerns, my love, respect, admiration, and sympathy with the Negro, and my love for my native South. Segregation is theologically, politically, and sociologically indefensible. It was a temporary expedient for the reconstitution of the white culture of the South and for the survival of millions of blacks who at the time were incapable of being assimilated into that culture. We learned to work together on a segregated basis, to respect and to love each other. Admittedly it is a structure that must come down. But will our civilization not be better off if this structure be taken down piece by piece, in an orderly manner, than it will be if the structure is blown suddenly to smithereens? The lawyer who reassured the reactionaries with the phrase "a century of litigation" has already been discredited by the events of less than ten years.

As a way of dramatizing his plight and of gaining support for his cause, the Negro has found a powerful weapon in demonstration. But it is a two-edged sword. Law and order must be upheld; the majesty of the law must be maintained. All right-thinking men have persistently deplored the abdication of peace officers in the face of the violence of vituperative white mobs, of governors of sovereign states disclaiming any power to cope with mob action, and so, in effect, inviting the mob to take over. Mass action cannot always be disciplined action. However just the cause, the mass may become a mob when discipline breaks down; the cause of justice may be forsworn in the call for revenge. The grave and present danger is that many persons sym-

pathetic to the Negro cause may prefer an ordered injustice to
the violence, discord, and confusion which could grow out of
general disrespect for law, another name for anarchy, or what
Louis Lomax has called "government by hell-raising."

Because I believe in the fatherhood of God, I believe in the
brotherhood of man. Because I believe in the brotherhood of
man, I believe society must offer "liberty and justice for all."
Because I believe in Christ as the son of God, and the saviour of
the world, I am certain that the gospel of Christ must be
preached to every creature. It makes me ashamed, therefore, to
recognize truth in the charge that our most segregated hour is
eleven o'clock of a Sunday morning.

As churchman and Christian, I am deeply repentant that our
conduct in local communities is so blatantly opposed to the
plain teachings of Christ, and to the equally plain pronouncements of the Church on racial matters. We cannot defend our
inaction on the ground that it is a difficult and complex problem
on which there is much to be said on both sides. It is a fact of
history, however, that the present situation has given rise to a
rebirth of southern racism which fifteen years ago most of us
thought dead and all but buried. Southern nationalism which
was more or less a joke is now a virulent and bitter disease in-
fecting not merely the old but the young. Even the liberal poli-
tician in the deep South feels he has to wave that flag if he expects to win elections.

It makes me sad to say that racism is not peculiar to our region, and that reactionaries and racists, North and South, could
make common cause against the aspirations of the Negro. Not
for one moment can our country, or the Church in our country
relinquish their insistence upon the goal of racial equality. Both
Church and country can, however, admonish all people to move
toward the goal in "mutual forbearance, fairness and good will."

Law cannot compel a man to get rid of his prejudice, but it
can compel him to act toward its object as if his prejudice did
not exist. Law cannot compel one man to associate with another,
but it can remove a major barrier against such association. Law

cannot compel me to recognize my neighbor's full humanity, but it can, by removing his disabilities, give me opportunity for discovering it.

People who have been denied full participation in the democratic process have a touching and naïve faith in the power of that process to eradicate evil, to accomplish the good. Others who have participated tend to be cynical, and content themselves with the more modest goal of ameliorating the effects of evil systems, of bettering the lot of the generality of man, of punishing the unjust and deterring him from the more blatant practice of injustice.

In the midst of World War II William Temple said, "We are not fighting for a better world, but for the chance to create that better world." When the world is free it is not necessarily better, but freedom does provide an atmosphere in which a better world may be forthcoming.

For the first time in American history we are challenged to give full freedom to all our citizens. If we meet that challenge we shall then be confronted with the more demanding challenge of accomplishing by means of our freedom such goals as peace, righteousness, justice, mutuality, brotherhood. These cannot be merely institutional and governmental, but must be personal and vocational. Moses led God's people into the promised land; Jesus Christ sent them out of it to create lands of promise throughout the world.

10. The Church and the Freedom Movement

JAMES P. BREEDEN

The Church now has another chance. There is a present and obvious crisis in race relations in the United States which opens up to the Church the opportunity to witness to the crisis of the Gospel: the effective end of dehumanizing separations among persons accomplished in Jesus Christ.

The "Negro Revolution," or "Freedom Movement," gives the Church a chance to acknowledge past unfaithfulness in penitence and to search the Scriptures and contemporary history seeking to follow the actions of its Lord. The presence of the Freedom Movement—which is to say the presence of the Negro —brings the Church face-to-face with the necessity of being concerned with the health of the whole social order, while being concerned with the good of the neighbor.

The Freedom Movement involves the whole of society. The impulse at its base is total; the Negro cannot be free until the white is free. The implications are, therefore, far more profound than any specific achievement might indicate. Only by God's grace may the true dimensions of that impulse be perceived. May the commitments and actions of the Church now be of such a character that it will be unable to settle back in comfort when a few token liberations will have been achieved.

The Church's participation in the Freedom Movement has followed the Movement itself to a new level. The 1963 Whitsuntide message of Presiding Bishop Lichtenberger of the Episcopal Church stated clearly and boldly the imperative for involvement in the struggle to secure the civil and human rights of all citizens of the United States. The Presiding Bishop's message went far beyond the sad and empty declarations of principle that have been so characteristic of the Church in the past, for it indicated appropriate action for Churchmen—action which covered the spectrum from civil disobedience to selective patronage, from negotiation to lobbying.

Yet the integrity of the Church is open to severe challenge. In the past, notice has been taken of the considerable gap between the high pronouncements of the Church and the impressive lack of bold action. In the past, it has been a fact that the Church has frequently provided leaders while its general day to day life remained without distinction.

The challenge to the Church's integrity goes deeper, however, for the Church is a segregated and segregating body. Such a body can only address itself boldly to the need for change in United States' society while addressing itself with equal boldness in word and deed to its own life. Christians ought not to be surprised that judgement begins with the household of God.

The Church is a segregated body. It is segregated by congregations which characteristically include or are dominated by one class or race. It is even more severely segregated by denominations. The Episcopal Church is unquestionably a "white Church." The Church's parochial schools, summer camps, office staffs, educational and promotional materials, by and large, fail to demonstrate an active concern for representing the inclusiveness of its faithful life. Were the practices of hiring clergy in most congregations open to the scrutiny of fair employment investigation, there are few vestries that could avoid indictment. In order to support its segregated life, the Church has developed the heretical gospel which proclaims that it is natural for people who are alike to be more comfortable together.

The Church is also a segregating body. Beyond more flagrant support and leadership given to segregationists' actions and institutions—less rare than one would hope—the Church participates in a segregated society without examining the character of that participation. The result is massive and unself-conscious support and sanction of unfaithful, dehumanizing separation. The Church invests money without regard for the employment practices or other economic involvements of the businesses its money supports. It builds new buildings without questioning the composition of the labor force which does the work. It locates new buildings in the center of racially and economically monolithic communities.

The Church must speak and act to bring the attention of United States' society to the Gospel. But the Church's own life is so inattentive to that very Gospel, it will be no wonder if both Church and Gospel are rejected by society, while both society and Church are rejected by our Lord!

The integrity of the Church is not substantially different in word or deed in the North and South. Clearly, as far as the Church's life is concerned, the division between North and South is as unfaithful and anti-catholic as the division by race and class.

It becomes increasingly apparent that the categories "North" and "South" are of less value in understanding the issues of desegregetion and integration than they were in a less honest time. To be sure, in the South, with its history of slavery and reconstruction, the presupposition of Negro inferiority is often reinforced by state and local law and by actions of public officials, in violation of federal law and policy. In the North, the same presupposition is reinforced by private action or veiled legal and political action in violation of state and local law, and in opposition to public policy. However, for the Negro, the South and the North are remarkably alike. The presupposition of Negro inferiority governs the institutions and the psychology of the United States as a whole. Going home at night to Harlem is no more subtle than going to the back of the bus.

The key city in the inner history of the Freedom Movement is a Southern one: Birmingham. It is significant, however, that Birmingham touched off large-scale direct action not only in the South but across the whole of the North as well. In general, it may be said that Birmingham began to break the back of the apathy, frustration, and bitterness of the Northern urban scene. Birmingham exposed the controls of fear that have chained the Negro in injustice. But Birmingham also exposed the weakness of fear as a control. Jail became a badge of honor, a new tool in the struggle for freedom, rather than a sign of victory for the forces of injustice. "Are you willing to go to jail for Freedom?" became the rallying cry of the entire Freedom Movement. The Church might well remember, then, as it has experienced from time to time in history, that jail is not an unfamiliar place to Christians.

The principal effect of Birmingham was a psychological one. To be a Negro in the United States, North or South, is to be persuaded openly and secretly that one is inferior. Moreover, it is to be persuaded that one is somehow guilty. Somehow the constant threat of indignities and injustices that our society imposes in the form of individual acts, traditional ways, and official policies is felt to be deserved. One ends up hating one's self. The control exercised by self-hatred is frequently powerful enough to keep the presupposition of Negro inferiority from being openly challenged. Yet in the background lies the "gentleman's agreement," the name lost in the file—"I'll call you if something opens up"—the jail cell, the police dog, the electric prod pole, the bomb.

To discover the perversity of the line of feeling and reason that leads to self-hatred is to discover the road to freedom. It is on the basis of this psychological discovery that the pain and danger of the penalties imposed and permitted by the majority can be faced. Negroes in the United States have been insulted, excluded, jailed, beaten, and killed for asserting their human and constitutional rights for more than three hundred years. In the Freedom Movement these things are occurring as part of a

large-scale revolution, however, and no longer as a series of isolated and largely unknown acts. For more than three hundred
years Negroes have been pointing out the contradiction between
the principles fought for in the American Revolution and the
practices based on the theory of Negro inferiority. For the first
time, however, our entire society is being forced to pay attention.
For the first time significant elements of the rest of our society
are beginning to join the cry.

The key event in the outer history of the Freedom Movement
is, of course, the *Brown* decision of the Supreme Court in May
of 1954. In this decision, for the first time the Negro American
was brought fully under the protection of the Constitution. Although the decision applied directly only to schools, it implicitly
challenged every institution and practice in United States' society based on the assumption of Negro inferiority.

Following the *Brown* decision, later actions by the Federal
courts have consistently upheld the principles of an integrated
society. The Executive and Legislative branches of the Federal
government have followed the Judicial lead cautiously and re-
luctantly, especially in the face of flagrant opposition by State
and local governments, business interests, and voluntary groups
such as White Citizen's Councils, the Klan, and some churches.
In spite of this lack of enthusiasm, however, the Federal Government has provided a permissive framework for revolutionary
change in our society. The Freedom Movement has supplied
and continues to supply a necessary part of the dynamic for that
change.

At its newest level, the principal mode of operation of the
Freedom Movement has been non-violent direct action. This involves the direct assertion of legal and moral rights with a willingness to bear the pain and inconvenience that may result from
doing so. As well, a loving concern is intended for those who
would seek to deny rights by violence or other means. Non-
violent direct action tends to expose the character of those forces
and persons that have previously maintained the institutions and
practices based on the premise of Negro inferiority. Non-violent

direct action gives persons the opportunity to participate directly in social change and thereby experience a measure of the human dignity long denied them. Finally, non-violence works.

Non-violent direct action depends in part for its effectiveness upon the permissive governmental framework in which the Freedom Movement now works. Most of the participants are not theologically or philosophically committed to non-violence as a way of life. Tangible results are important. Thus the continuation of non-violence as the dominant form of direct action depends in part upon the continuation and acceleration of the rate of desegregation. There is a real possibility inherent in the current situation that the economic and political structure of the United States may prove to be more intransigent than it is hoped to be. If this proves to be the case, we can expect a general alienation of the Negro from our society, with the possibility of a shift to violent methods, governmental repression of the Freedom Movement, and a time of extreme moral decay. Such a circumstance could well ring the death knell for our society.

The Church has another chance. One aspect has to do with cleansing its own life, while constructively criticising and changing the wider community. A second aspect has to do with the participation of its members in the Freedom Movement at all levels of the revolution.

The Christian is already committed to an integrated society by virtue of his baptism into the integrated community which is the faithful Church. It is the privilege of the Christian to spell out that commitment in the words and acts of life.

Given the depths of the separation within the Church and within our society, one of the first options for the Christian is to become an active member in a congregation which represents a racial, cultural, or class composition different from his own. Further, in choosing a place to live, one must recognize the unnatural divisions which tend to separate the Christian from his neighbors. The white Christian may freely move into the ghetto of the black and the poor. The black Christian has a responsibility to move into the white ghetto and a right to expect that at least some of his neighbors will share the burdens this may impose upon him and his family.

In the economic sphere, one who is an employer must act to seek out the underemployed and the unemployed. The investor and the consumer must be aware of the social effects of the economic interests they support with their money, and be willing to withdraw their support from those who refuse to pursue economic policies that benefit the whole community.

In the political area, the Christian must be aware of the total community welfare. He must take an active part in the whole elective process. He must seek to influence his representatives to act responsibly, by letter and personal confrontation.

Finally, the Christian must be active and informed in the field of civil rights. Simply in the area of information, it is important to realize that one cannot get a true picture of the Freedom Movement from the white press. When a local Negro newspaper or magazine exists, one ought to read it regularly. Some of the civil rights organizations put out regular publications. A number of weekly newspapers have regional and national coverage. These publications are a minimal "must."

The Freedom Movement is exposing a deep sickness in the soul of United States' society, in the life of the Church, in the heart of man. No interpretation, explanation, or exhortation can prevent or adequately prepare us for confrontation with that sickness. Our certain hope is the assurance that in this time of great danger and promise our Lord is mightily at work among us and calls us now, as always, to be his faithful witnesses.

11. The Days Are Coming—A Sermon

DUNCAN M. GRAY, JR.

The prophet Amos was a simple herdsman from the tiny Judean village of Tekoa, but there burned within him a passion for social justice and righteousness the like of which has not often appeared in the history of the world. To see a nation which professed such devotion to God so rife with economic and political injustice and oppression was more than he could stand, and he thundered out his protest in the name of a righteous God. His prophetic message of judgement was directed primarily at the ruling class of Israel, including the king himself. It was no wonder, then, that his message was not kindly received by those in power; and it was not long before he was driven out of the country. As best we can tell, his ministry lasted only about three months.

With this in mind, it might seem a bit strange to read of the judgement promised in our text: " 'Behold, the days are coming,' says the Lord God, 'when I will send a famine on the land; not a famine of bread, nor a thirst for water, but of hearing the words of the Lord' " (Amos 8:11, RSV). It might seem to us that nothing would have pleased the leaders of Israel more than just this. If the word of the Lord could be silenced—if the voice of His prophets could be stilled—then those in power could go on exploiting the poor and oppressing the needy to their own advantage. There would be no public voice of conscience, no confrontation with God, to deter them from their evil ways.

To hear the word of the Lord is not always a pleasant thing. Surely, there have been times in our lives when we might have devoutly wished that the voice of God could be silenced; that we would not have to *hear* the demands made upon us by the faith to which we are committed. Job gives this feeling classic expression as he ponders his own situation and cries out to God:

> Let me alone, for my days are a breath
> What is man, that thou dost make so much of him, and
>   that thou dost set thy mind upon him, dost visit him every
>   morning, and test him every moment?
> How long wilt thou not look away from me, nor let me
>   alone till I swallow my spittle?
> If I sin, what do I do to thee, thou watcher of men?
> Why hast thou made me thy mark?
> Why have I become a burden to thee?
>
> (Job 7:16b-20, RSV)

"Let me alone!" How often this might be our own most fervent prayer to the God who made us. How simple and easy life might sometime be if God would leave us alone—if words such as love and duty, righteousness and justice, held no final content apart from what we ourselves chose to make of them! Life would be so much easier if it were simply my own to do with as I pleased, without reference to God or man, except as I might see fit to make such reference apply. Surely, this must be the hidden, though perhaps unconscious, motive behind much of the indifference toward religion which we encounter on every side; and it is a motive which we should be able to understand. A life of ultimate irresponsibility does have a real appeal. How much easier it might be if we did not have to hear the word of the Lord!

And yet, it is God's word of judgement addressed to us and our capacity to receive it that distinguishes us from the other animals. It is God's word of judgement and our capacity to hear it that mark us as responsible creatures: creatures answerable for our words and deeds, because we are not merely the product of natural forces beyond our control, but free beings capable of God's judgement is what gives hope and meaning to our lives; it says that what we say and do here and now matters ultimately. Therefore, a famine of hearing God's word of judgement, such as Amos promised Israel, would be the worst thing that could befall us. We must not have such a famine, no matter how attractive the prospect might sound at times.

God's word of judgement has not changed since the days of Amos and Job. God still stands over against us and over against our society, speaking to us of what we are, as compared with that which we were created to be. He stands in judgement upon our self-centeredness; upon our tendency to make ourselves the center of meaning and our own preferences and prejudices the final criteria for right and wrong, good and evil. He stands in judgement upon our misuse of the gifts which He has given us, from the soil of the good earth to the mysteries of nuclear energy. He stands in judgement upon our failure to live as brothers one of another, in the community, in the nation, and in the world. And we must hear His word of judgement, if we are not to give up our very humanity. We must hear His word of judgement lest we forget and forego our responsibility—our answerability—which lends the dimension of meaning to our lives here and now.

God's word of judgement has not changed since the days of Amos and Job. But since that time, God has spoken to us another word as well; a word which comes from the Cross. In one sense, this word is the severest judgement of all; for it reveals to us in concrete and tangible terms the way God fares when He comes into this world of ours. We nail Him to a Cross. But this is not the final word. For on the Cross God has taken His place beside us. He has shared our predicament with us. In Christ, God has taken upon Himself our sins and their consequences. He shares the judgement with us so that we may face His judgement unafraid. The final word from the Cross is one of pardon and grace and strength to endure.

And it is this word from the Cross that makes it possible for us to hear God's word of judgement without falling into the pit of despair. Without the Cross, we could hardly be blamed for avoiding and evading the word of the Lord as it is spoken by men such as Amos. Such a word is too much for us to bear; too much for us to live with. We find that we must evade it, modify it, or simply give in to hopelessness and despair. But with God's word from the Cross, all this is changed. Knowing the mercy and grace that comes from the Cross, we can find the strength and the courage to face up to our sins and to respond creatively to God's judgement upon them.

I think it is especially important that, as a Church, we keep this very much in mind during the days and months ahead, as we hear and pronounce God's word of judgement upon the grievous sins of racial injustice and discrimination. I come from a part of the country where our burden of guilt in these matters is particularly heavy. (And it is a burden, even for many of those who would most vehemently deny it. A deep-seated sense of guilt manifests itself in a variety of ways, not the most unusual of which is a passionate and even violent denial of guilt.) But precisely because the guilt of the white South is so great, it is doubly hard for us to *hear* and to *accept* God's word of judgement. This is a judgement which veritably shakes the foundations, not just of a sinful, man-made society, but of the individual psyche as well. It is not an easy thing for the average white Southerner to face.

The point I would make, though, is that he can never face it in a meaningful and creative way, unless he hears and knows from the other side of that word of judgement God's word from the Cross. We cannot receive and accept God's word in an Amos until we also hear God's word in Christ. And so the Church, along with her essential and crucial prophetic ministry, has another equally important ministry to fulfil: the ministry of reconciliation. Laws and institutions can be *reformed*—and this we must do with all haste—but people must be *redeemed*. Redemption, in the final analysis, is the fruit of love; the fruit of a love so great that it takes the sin of the sinner upon itself and shares the judgement with him. It is God's business to redeem; but it is the Church's business to be His instrument of redemption. This we do, not by speaking God's word of judgement from some lofty pinnacle of self-righteousness, but by taking our place in love and compassion alongside the sinner where we know that the judgement falls upon us as well as upon him.

In this connection, I would like to paraphrase a few words of Will Campbell, a native white Mississippian and a fellow Churchman. In his book *Race and the Renewal of the Church*,[1] he says—and I would say with him: "I have seen and known the resentment of the racist, his hostility, his frustration, his need for someone upon whom to lay blame and to punish. I know he is mistaken, misguided, and willfully disobedient, but somehow, *I am not able to distinguish between him and myself.* My sins may not be his sins, but they are no less real and no less serious. Perhaps I have been too close to this man. Perhaps if I had not heard his anguished cry when the rains didn't come in time to save his cotton; if I had not felt the severity of his economic deprivation; if I had not shared his joys and his sorrows in birth and death, in success and failure; if I had not been one with him in so many gales of tragedy, I would be able to condemn him without hesitation. If I had not shared his plight; if I had not lived with him in an atmosphere of suspicion, distrust, ignorance, misinformation, and nefarious political leadership, surely my heart would break less when I see him fomenting mob violence in front of his school and his church. Perhaps I would not pity him and love him as I do, if I were not a part of him. But pity and love him I do."

My own state, my own community, my own church have known and felt the judgement of God—whether or not we have recognized it as such—and we will feel it many times more before justice is done. It is not a pleasant experience. But every real encounter with God begins with His judgement upon us; and within each such encounter is always the potential for grace. This the white Southerner must be made to see and to understand. For he cannot really hear and respond to God's shattering word of judgement, until he also hears that word of saving grace which comes from the Cross. And he must hear both of these words in and through his Church.

There must be no famine of hearing the word of the Lord in our land today. The Negro has suffered far too long and far too much; and by now we should all be aware of how late is the hour and how urgent is the need to abolish all forms of discrimination based upon the color of a man's skin. It is a time when the Church must speak God's word of judgement with relevance and power; particularly since she has failed so conspicuously to do so in the past. You and I must speak this word with such insistence and such power that it will penetrate the heart and soul of every man, woman, and child in America today. But we must never do so in such a way as to drown out the other word that comes from the Cross. For it is in that word that our ultimate salvation lies. The Church has a mission to judge; but in fulfilling that mission, she must never lose the will and the power to *redeem*.

NOTES

[1] Adapted from *Race and Renewal of the Church* by Will D. Campbell. Copyright © 1962, W. L. Jenkins. The Westminster Press. Used by permission.

12. Unity

GEORGE W. WICKERSHAM, II

It is no strange thing that the issue of unity looms large in the Church today. The world has been so shrunk by the incredible speed of modern modes of transport that nobody is more than twenty-four hours from anybody else. This is a world in which unity of all sorts, economic, political, social, is bound to be a major issue. Further, we have in our hands instruments to effect unity: telephone, radio, television, a press with a vast international organization, plus a plethora of recording and duplicating devices; these make it all but impossible for a human being to remain uninformed as to what others are thinking and doing. Need I add that the move towards unity among men has the added goad of the bomb? To the call of Heaven is added the fear of Hell, whether or not fear is ever an effective stimulus to love.

When all this is said, however, it must be remembered that as far as the Church is concerned, unity is no recent issue. One might reasonably argue that it has always been the great issue of Christianity. "You shall love the Lord your God with all your heart, and with all your soul, and with all your mind. This is the great and first commandment. And a second is like it, You shall love your neighbor as yourself. On these two commandments depend all the law and the prophets" (Matt. 22:37-40, RSV).

In the face of this, the Christian religion is presented to the world by literally hundreds of different groups, few of which have been willing to give more than polite acknowledgment to any of the others. This is what is often referred to as the "scandal of disunity in the Church." The general public accepts it as an accomplished fact, but there is no doubt in my mind that it is the greatest single deterrent to the spread of the Gospel. What it actually means is that those who profess to hear the Gospel have never learned to apply it to more than a limited number of their relationships. "So if you are offering your gift at the altar, and there remember that your brother has something against you, leave your gift there before the altar and go; first be reconciled to your brother, and then come and offer your gift" (Matt. 5:23-24, RSV). From this it seems obvious that unity must be our number one objective in the Church.

This is not to say that there will not always be brethren who simply will not be reconciled; but over two hundred and fifty large denominations in the United States alone would appear to reveal a patent lack of proper efforts towards reconciliation.

That such a condition should exist is actually all but inexplicable. It can only be labelled as one of the great monuments to human folly. All of these groups, with one or two exceptions, hold equally fast to the most uniting of all convictions, namely, the belief that God so loved the world that He sent His Son. What, then, can so divide us? If Christ has "broken down the dividing wall of hostility . . ." (Eph. 2:14, RSV), why is it still there? Here we must get technical (which is, I believe, revelation enough of the reasons for the continued existence of the wall). We are still floundering around in religions of law, unable to comprehend more than a measure of the new religion of Grace; and it is, after all, very new.

On the night when He was betrayed, Jesus "took bread, and when he had given thanks, he broke it, and said, 'This is my body which is for you. Do this in remembrance of me.' In the same way also the cup, after supper, saying, 'This cup is the new covenant in my blood. Do this, as often as you drink it, in remembrance of me' " (I Cor. 11:23-25, RSV). St. Paul adds that as often as we eat this bread and drink the cup, we proclaim the Lord's death until He comes.

One would think this to be rather enough to cause us to bury the hatchet. Actually it has occasioned unbelievable wrangling. Who is to perform this rite? When? Where? And what are we to believe about it?

I often wonder whether our Lord would have instituted His Supper had He known of the bitterness which was to grow up around it. That St. John omitted it from his narrative and told of the foot-washing instead has always appeared to me as somehow significant.

At any rate, few seem yet inclined simply to take Jesus at His word and "do" what He commanded, which is, after all, of the essence of a sacrament, and which would indeed bring us together everywhere, anywhere. No, we have to legalize. We are told that only those properly authorized may "do" this thing, and that only those properly indoctrinated may partake of it. The Church might just as well have retained circumcision.

In the Protestant Episcopal Church this issue comes to a head in the fourth point of the Lambeth Quadrilateral, a four-point platform put forth by Anglican Bishops as the basis for uniting with other Christian bodies. The first three points are accepted by almost all churches: the Bible, the Creeds, the two Sacraments of Baptism and Holy Communion. The fourth, the Ministry of Bishops, Priests and Deacons in Apostolic Succession, is a stumbling block to many of them. Not that they disapprove, but rather that they sense a strong feeling on the part of many Episcopalians that all other ministries have been and are "invalid." When the matter is discussed, this alleged lack of validity always seems to find its focal point at the Communion Table.

Here the question of belief as to what the Communion means becomes the issue, and we are "in deep." But are we in something in which we ought to be? Is the issue itself a valid one?

The Roman Catholic Church is faced with this tremendous

question, and from the recent great events in Rome one derives
a strong impression that the late Pope John XXIII did some
thinking far deeper than that of many of history's most noted
divines.

Those who hold "high" views of the second Sacrament feel
the need for official channels of Grace thru which the miracle
of the Mass may be implemented. Love, however, is still the
imperative of a Christian. Since all Christians agree that love
is not possible in a human being without Divine Grace, and
since love is found here and there in all denominational families,
one begins to sense that Grace by-passes the so-called proper
channels with some frequency.

During the Second World War, the United States had half a
million men on the island of Saipan in the Pacific. I was Protestant Chaplain to three thousand of them. Outfits dotted the
seventeen-mile island. Transports arrived with additions almost
daily. One of them was possessed of a zealous Episcopal Chaplain
whose mission in life was to sort out fellow Episcopalians on his
ship, list their names, and forward the lists to me. Apparently I
was to seek these men out in the labyrinth of Army, Army Air
Force, Navy, and Marine units on the island and save their souls
from contamination by non-Episcopal Chaplains.

It was my strong feeling, however, that these men could exercise their Christianity far more effectively by worshipping God
with the men of their own outfits, even if this meant such a
horrendous thing as attending Roman Mass. This alone appeared
to me as "valid."

Therefore if our doctrine of the Christian Ministry is separating us from our Christian brothers, I would say that the time
has come for us to question its validity. "For no other foundation
can anyone lay than that which is laid, which is Jesus Christ"
(I Cor. 3:11, RSV).

What happens when you unite with other churches on the
basis of the "one foundation" only? Episcopalians are trying this
at Indian Hill, Ohio, in Ashfield, Massachusetts, and in Tamworth, New Hampshire. This last project involves a Baptist

church, a Congregational church (United Church of Christ)
and a Protestant Episcopal church. Each little church is in a
separate community, but all are in the same town. I am Town
Minister and, as such, in charge of all three. There is an element
of "phoneyness" to our ecumenicity, since the current agreement
prescribes that the Minister always be an Episcopalian. To Episcopalians it seems obvious that the Minister of an Episcopal
church must be an Episcopalian. It is not at all obvious to Baptists or to Congregationalists; but to their everlasting credit, they
have accepted it in Tamworth. This they did, not because they
suddenly embraced episcopacy, but because they had more desire
for unity than has the Episcopal Church. And what is the result?
The young people of Tamworth are growing up in the belief
that they are all members one of another, rather than of separated
groups. I cannot imagine a more thrilling process to behold.

There is to the Christian religion a tremendous centripetal
pull. Unity will always be its central issue. In spite of this, there
will always be those in the Church who oppose unity, and for
obvious reasons. Some have positions of authority which are
jeopardized by mergers. Some cannot see out of the rut in which
they have been running for so long. Some have an almost compulsive need to be in an exclusive group. There will be those also
whose reasons for opposing larger fellowship are not so obvious.
They will talk at great length on the subject of "truth." Still,
the only real Christian truth is love. "I am the way, and the
truth, and the life . . ." (John 14:6, RSV).

The doctrine of transubstantiation appears to require a priestly
caste empowered to change the elements, although even this is
open to question. Apart from this, however, there is still much
to be said for a continuous line of Bishops, especially if there
are democratic checks and balances on their authority. To say
this is one thing. To say, "No Bishop, no Church," is quite another. The reason why we have the Tamworth Plan at all is
that those of us on the Episcopal side in that mountain parish
do not believe any such proposition.

Which brings me to what I consider to be the major point in

any unity movement. Christ is the only valid foundation for the Church. When we insist on anything else, we are simply building walls, not temples.

If Bishops continue to divide us, should we be willing to abolish Bishops? I am sure that God would not thereupon abandon the Church. On the other hand, I am equally sure that if we were willing to dispense with them, Bishops would be back in less than a week's time. Witness the non-Episcopal churches today. Almost all of them have Bishops. They give them other titles. Their duties are lacking some of those pertaining to Episcopal Bishops. Episcopal Bishops are lacking some of theirs. I know a good deal about these non-Episcopal Bishops. I have two. They are pastors' Pastors. Like Episcopal Bishops, they go about their dioceses doing good, and, also like Episcopal Bishops, they sit at their desks doing not-so-good. In all probability, many of them would like to be Episcopalians. It is the apparent absolutism of our dogma about Bishops which makes them hesitate. I am just Episcopalian enough to believe that most people would be Episcopalian were it not for us Episcopalians.

Having thus dealt somewhat bluntly with the Order of Bishops, we would do well to recognize that there may be to this ancient office a hidden factor which has much to do with the subject at hand: unity.

It is most interesting to note that Pope John XXIII placed high among the objectives of the Second Vatican Council an increased emphasis on the importance of the Order of Bishops.

There is little doubt in my mind that one of the motives behind this move stems from the fact that the Pope saw in Bishops a possible source of unity with the other churches. Bishops have been found a source of reunion between churches in India, and, in spite of all that we have said heretofore, they are being found a possible source of unity among at least some of the various churches in the United States and Australia.

It could be that Bishops will provide the mortar between the bricks of the coming great Church.

What strikes me as of particular importance to those of us

who are already in churches with an episcopal polity is that we should bear in mind that Bishops may well be mortar, but never foundation.

The issue of unity can be measured only by the size of our hearts. God is, after all, a Spirit. I have come to dread hearing my parishioners in Tamworth use the words "Episcopal," "Baptist" or "Congregational" any more. Even though each word denotes a tradition which may have much to contribute, these labels have been divisive factors too long. I rejoice to hear Tamworth citizens speak of "the Church." When they do, I am quick to catch overtones of respect. And those overtones are there. Why? Simply because our three churches, in their present association, are at least giving some official evidence of practicing what they preach: love.

The doctrine, polity, and effectiveness of the Tamworth Associated Churches depend in large measure upon how sincere its members are in their Christian concern for people.

When all the theological treatises are signed, sealed and delivered, you and I can be sure that much of the doctrine, most of the polity, and all of the effectiveness of the Church at large will depend on the concern of its members for reaching out in Christ's name to all of God's dispersed children.

When we want unity, its many problems will fade away.

13. Missionary Frontiers in Our Midst

WALTER D. DENNIS

It has been said that the Episcopal Church never attempted to reach the Western frontier in America until Pullman coaches arrived on the transportation scene to transport its missionaries there, and, by that time, the people on the edge of settlement were already lost to those denominations which arrived there "firstest with the mostest."

Missionary activity of the Episcopal Church in this country got off to a very slow start indeed. Certainly because we were a "Johnny-come-lately" church in the field of missionary endeavor, we have suffered enormously to this day as a consequence. The churches which christianized the great areas of the West where America was expanding in colonial times shaped the denominational pattern in America which has lasted to our own times. Moreover, the Protestant churches which captured the missionary field at that point have remained ahead and even dominated the thinking of the other churches.

The Living Church Quarterly of 1890 showed that the Episcopal Church had 48,596 communicants in the region lying between the Mississippi River and the states and territories on the Pacific Coast. On the Pacific Coast in 1890 there were 11,197 communicants divided among two dioceses, California and Oregon, and two missionary jurisdictions, Northern California and Washington. As the total number of communicants in the Epis-

copal Church in the continental United States in 1890 was
484,020, the number on the Pacific Coast represented two per
cent of the strength of the Church, and those in the interior
east to the Mississippi represented ten per cent. Even though the
Census Bureau said that the frontier was closed, the Episcopal
Church continued to act as if it weren't, simply because the
domestic strategy of the whole previous century had been formulated and predicated upon the assumption that new work should
be created along geographical lines. With the exception of work
among American Indians and Negroes, Domestic Missions in
the twentieth century in the Episcopal Church continued to be
formulated along geographical lines.

Probably the first deviation from this policy was the creation,
in 1936, by a small group of laymen and clergy, of the Church
Society for College Work. Its purpose was to alert the Church
to the fact that work among college students and faculty was
a mission field—although not a geographical one—and that it
deserved the whole Church's attention and support. Since that
time we have seen the establishment of work among the Deaf
and Blind, the Aged, Migrant Workers and Immigrants, among
the Armed Forces, as part of the concern for Domestic Missions.

What has been less clearly seen is a unique opportunity to
be in the vanguard of the Church's mission to the urban frontier.
The 1920 census established that the United States was more
urban than rural, and, since that time, it has become increasingly
clear that urbanization is to affect all facets of American life—
rural and urban alike. Even when the Episcopal Church tardily
moved to the frontier, it never left the urban, and has always
been for the most part an urban church. For this reason it
should draw upon its repository of experience in the urban centers rather than abandon the cities for more comfortable existence in suburbia and exurbia. Maybe the Episcopal Church has
survived primarily in the city all these years in preparation for
just such an historic occasion as that which the next century or
so of urbanization will most certainly bring forth.

So the Episcopal Church, because it is an urban church, can

set itself pre-eminently to the task of attracting the urban seeker, of ministering to those religiously disaffected city dwellers who these days are more open to religion. Formerly, the Church in its domestic policy subscribed to a geographical and parochial line; now it must act boldly and imaginatively on the intellectual and cultural frontier that urban society demands of it.

Christians must see the inner-city as a mission field and, as such, face foursquare the problems there of race and cultural conflicts. This may mean in some instances that we must give more attention to American Indians moving to the cities than to those currently living on Reservations. It may mean that we will have to follow the lead of, and give support to, more housing clinics such as the one established by the Church of St. Matthew and St. Timothy in New York City, where many people of that neighborhood bring their problems and complaints.

Through that clinic the clergy and workers seek to force landlords to obey the housing and building regulations, to charge fair rents, and to keep their buildings in order. Morever, the clinic attempts to impress upon the tenants the importance of their part in maintaining the condition of the buildings in which they live. As more and more people move from rural areas to urban places, there will be even greater need for the Church to undertake this kind of neighborhood work as an expression of its concern for people.

In some instances we must go "beyond the fringe" and establish places such as the Village Aid and Service Center which is operated by the Judson Memorial Church in Greenwich Village, New York, to aid narcotics addicts. In so doing we will be witnessing to the fact that there is no corner of human existence into which the church cannot venture.

Our attempts to minister on the newest frontiers must be discharged not only through programs of direct action but also through conferences for clergy and laymen and for the public at large on problems of urbanization. Happily, a beginning has already been made with a series of conferences called "Metabag-

dad" on the spectrum of urban problems in the great metropolitan complexes.

At the same time we must also give encouragement to those
forms of artistic expression, such as drama, music and art, which
have been the historic heritage of the Church. Unfortunately
we have only scratched the surface in the second area in trying
to minister to the urban frontier. But at St. Clement's Episcopal
Church in New York City, drama is now emerging as a vital
means of communication for that church. Because of its location in the theatre district, the priest-in-charge has Sunday services at noon to encourage the attendance of actors and actresses.
Recently a scene from the play *Look Back in Anger* was presented before the regular service began and, on another Sunday,
The Last Word was presented in place of a sermon. The
clergy have indicated that they hope to create at St. Clement's
"a place that inspires, fosters and produces written works for a
theatre that concerns itself with the critical themes of contemporary life." This is but one way that a church has updated in
an imaginative way the religious use of drama and made it a
tool for ministering to the twentieth century urban frontier.

Another church in the New York City area which is sensitive
to its urban responsibility is St. Mark's in the Bowerie. Recently
this church sponsored a fine arts festival displaying the talents
of young artists, dancers, and writers. Similar undertakings have
been initiated at Grace Cathedral, San Francisco. This ministry
to the arts suggests a few ways that the Church can express the
bearing of the Christian faith into every aspect of human life in
an increasingly urbanized society.

If the Church does not deal with such problems as alcoholism,
the aging, and homosexuality now, it may not have the opportunity later to do so. In order to exercise this ministry the
Church must find new ways and means to break through into
what used to be taboo areas, seeing them as the latest frontier.
Even if, in some instances, the Church finds that it cannot rally
general support for these unpopular causes, it will have shown
itself willing to help those who have been "unequally yoked."

For example, Dr. Alfred A. Gross of the George W. Henry Foundation has pleaded in his latest book, *Strangers in Our Midst*, for the Church to provide leadership in helping people cope with problems of homosexuality. Since it is well settled that guilt arising out of such relationships is submerged by layers of sophistication and cannot be relieved even by an inordinate amount of counseling, it may be that the Church must make use of its disciplined latent homosexuals in carrying a Christian witness to guilt-ridden homosexuals. Properly handled and understood, this could be a real contribution to the furtherance of the Church's mission in particular artistic sections and in areas such as the Beatnik fringe. What is suggested here in the realm of homosexuality could also be initiated—with adaptation—in dealing with aberrations such as alcoholism, dope addiction, and other problems in fractured parts of our society.

Therefore in this century, as always, the missionary task is to hold up before all the broken parts of Christ's Church on earth the image of One Holy Catholic Church. The Mission of the Church is to tie the eternal verities into the deep concerns and thought forms of contemporary man. God translated himself into a human life. Thus we must express the relevance of the Christian Faith in every realm—this will sometimes be on the beach at Fort Lauderdale, and at another time, in the midst of a Black Muslim rally in the middle of Harlem.

But the Gospel must be understood as relevant to each man, and the Church must provide the resources for interpretation of everything from the Theatre of the Absurd to Glossolalia. In the execution of this ministry, we must not attempt to return to the pattern of an earlier day. That would mean an effort doomed for failure. Rather we must seek to occupy the newest frontiers in vital and creative ways, attempting spiritual strides which no previous generation has known or even imagined.

14. What Constitutes a Missionary Opportunity?

CHARLES H. LONG, JR.

"I am sitting here on Mt. Olympus, wondering where in the world I can dispose of my inestimable gifts." So wrote a young missionary in China after the communist victory cut short what he expected to be a life-time career in the Far East. The Olympian attitude is slightly ridiculous when assumed by an individual, but in determining missionary strategy for the Church, such an attitude is simply taken for granted. There is supposed to be some way by which "they" (meaning the Bishops or the people at church headquarters) can gather all the facts concerning the secular and religious situation in every part of the world, determine what is the area of greatest need or opportunity, and then marshal men and money at that point, even if it means closing up less productive work elsewhere.

This is the way that business empires and political empires are both built up and maintained. It assumes that foreign missions *are* an expression of religious imperialism. It also assumes that the main object of foreign missions is the building up of the institutional Church—in a form, an outward and functional form, as much like our own as possible. Of course we must accommodate ourselves, to some extent, to such factors as the inadequacies of languages other than English, the child-like customs of the local people, the irrational nationalism found in so many foreign countries and the baffling inability of churches thus established to achieve what we call self-support. It takes time to overcome problems like these. But at least the Church has been established where it did not exist before, the Word and Sacraments are now available to those who were without them, another area of darkness has been penetrated, and more nations than ever before can be colored on our maps in blue to show that they belong to "our" side.

This is caricature, to be sure, but only partly so. Ideas like these, and the unconscious assumptions behind them, reflect much of the continuing and persistent mythology of foreign missions. The end of the Colonial era has not meant the end of imperialism, any more than the end of slavery has meant the end of racial discrimination. "The great need of the Churches in the West today is for an adequate expression in missionary structures of their new political and social relations with the peoples and Churches of Asia and Africa." [1] Much of our present confusion is due to failure to come to grips with the significance of the change that has already taken place.

There is no lack of suggestions for adapting 19th century missionary structures to 20th century use. Some would alter nomenclature, changing the term "missionary" to "fraternal worker" to emphasize a sense of "partnership" between "older" and "younger" churches. A Board of Foreign Missions prefers now to be known as a Board of "Overseas" or "Ecumenical" Mission, or even a "Division of World Ministries." Others stress the need for changing the attitudes of missionaries themselves, encouraging them to identify with the people among whom they live (without of course "going native" or giving up their American passports and furlough privileges), and to adapt themselves to a simpler standard of living, patterned more on the living standards of the people they serve than on those of American businessmen and government officials abroad. Others call for changes in missionary administration, decentralization of responsibility, more rapid development of an indigenous clergy, a change of emphasis from expensive educational and medical work to strengthening the Church itself, better promotion and "missionary education" through various schemes to "personalize" the program of the Church in distant lands.

Do any of these efforts to patch up the situation go far enough? They are certainly desirable reforms as far as they go. The past twenty years have seen extraordinary efforts on the part of the churches to change the image of foreign missions both in the minds of supporters at home and in the eyes of the beneficiaries of the program abroad. It must be admitted that these efforts have had only limited success. No amount of tinkering will adapt the horse and buggy to provide suitable transportation for our day. When one contemplates most of the so-called criticisms of the contemporary foreign missionary program and the "bold experiments" proposed to remedy its weaknesses, one is reminded of the remark by a contemporary novelist to the effect that the *avant-garde* is all too often no more than a rear guard.[2]

I believe that God is calling the Church to a *fundamental* change in its missionary orientation. Proposed reforms which do not probe deeply enough are like ever louder exhortations pitched in a shrill and almost desperate key. They are a disservice to the cause of mission because they help to maintain a little longer the illusion that the missionary enterprise of the past can somehow be preserved, and that the situation requires only a few adjustments in the machinery or a bit greater effort on the part of the white man in order to carry his burden further.

Hendrik Kraemer, one of the most respected missionary scholars of our day, is more forthright. After pointing out that the foreign missionary movement as we know it is a relatively recent development in Church history, and a movement inextricably linked to the structures and attitudes of Colonialism, he concludes, "Now it must be stated with the strongest possible emphasis that *in principle, though far from in fact, this whole* (missionary) *structure collapsed as a result of the second world war and its dramatic consequences. In this sense it is fully true that the 'era of missions has passed'—irrevocably.*"[3]

This has happened 'in principle' but not everywhere 'in fact.' In some places, such as China and the Sudan, it has clearly happened in fact, and not even a further revolutionary change of government will restore the missionary movement to a *status quo ante*. In other parts of the world, notably in Latin America and in much of Africa, traditional missionary and church work continues, despite radical changes in society and in international relations which proclaim the dawn of a new day. The degree of awareness towards, and willingness to adjust to, new social conditions varies, of course, from church to church and from individual to individual. There are exceptional cases of pioneer evangelism among primitive tribes in which there is no revolution to fear, because the initiation of social change appears to be, or is thought to be, entirely in the hands of missionaries themselves. On the whole, however, it is generally recognized that missionary patterns, structure, and strategy are going through a period of chaotic transition, accompanied by frustration and uncertainty on the part of everyone concerned.

Increasingly the Church is becoming concerned with its own defense. This can be seen in the rather fruitless attempts to find new and appropriate concepts of the term "frontier." In the aggressive days of missionary expansion, missionary frontiers were described in geographical terms, separating Christian from non-Christian countries, or, in each new nation claimed for Christ, unchurched territories from places where the church in some form was established. The frontier in this sense represented a clearly defined boundary or barrier which had to be *crossed* if those who were outside the Church were to be won into its fellowship.

Newer definitions of mission show the concept of frontier as a point of *engagement* between the Church and the World, a line to be held at all costs, an outpost to be defended. Canon Milford, several years ago, foresaw the need for bands of missionaries who would be prepared to sacrifice everything and undertake the most severe discipline to become "hedgehogs of the Christian way in heathen and hostile surroundings." Bishop

Newbigin writes of "the frontier between faith and unbelief" found in every part of the world, as the only true indicator of the line between the Church itself and the field of its mission. A Swiss theologian, Marc Spindler defines the new missionary frontier in these terms: "As Foreign Missions once planted the Church within the geographical areas which were discovered by the great Navigators (of the age of exploration), so now it is a matter of planting the Church in 'abstract areas' discovered by sociologists and economists." [4]

So we find the focus shifting from "that which lies beyond the boundary of Western civilization" to "that which lies beyond the boundary of the Church," until finally it is asked whether the line should not be drawn within the Church itself, between those who are faithful and those who are not. The phenomenal rise of Pentecostal movements and other holiness sects is an illustration of this last. The churches everywhere find the World pressing in upon them. In the new nations of Asia, Africa and Latin America they find themselves fighting for their sociological survival, as tiny minorities, facing overwhelming political and economic problems. Western churches feel that they have lost the initiative both at home and abroad to rival forces: communism, secularism, Mohammedism, etc. They see as never before the need for re-evangelization of their own lands. They are infected by the anxieties and defense-mindedness of the whole post-war period.

It is not surprising that churches have lost confidence in themselves as they recognize wide-spread worldliness, nominal faith, and social injustice at the very heart of what they once considered strong centers of their life and work. It is not surprising that foreign missionaries are also in many instances disillusioned and demoralized, not so much by the difficulties they face abroad, as by the inner conflict of trying to represent a home base which they inwardly and deeply criticize. In this they are supported by the unprecedented self-criticism which characterizes the very churches which send them out.

Recruitment for Church vocations reflects the same defensive posture. Those who a generation ago would have recognized the priority of foreign missionary frontiers are today more concerned about the "abstract frontiers" of urban evangelization, religious education, student work and pastoral psychotherapy. Western Christians are more willing to commit men and resources to the strengthening and expansion of the church they know, and whose weaknesses contemporary history has pitilessly revealed, than to send men and money to churches they do not know, and to missions which seem losing causes in distant places.

No one can deny the validity of these calls to rebuild the Church at its points of weakness in a hostile world, because they reflect the Church's rediscovery of an ultimate frontier within itself. The ultimate frontier is not between Man and Man (let alone between continent and continent, or abstraction and abstraction), but *between Man and God*. The relative frontiers that separate men, whether defined geographically, sociologically or ecclesiastically, are negations of every human claim to absolute or universal power, negations of every claim of man to be God. The ultimate frontier is one that only God is able to transcend or break down. It is our faith that He has already done so, that He has abolished this barrier through His mighty acts in Christ Jesus.

Every mission of the Church is determined, therefore, by the prior mission and ministry of Jesus Christ to the world. Mission does not begin with the recognition that we are sent to the foreigners; it begins with a recognition that in our separation and reconciliation through God's action in Christ we are one *with* the foreigners. We ourselves are the barbarians, the outcast, the heathen, the uncivilized to whom Christ has come. It is precisely because we know that when we were thus alienated from Him, God so loved us that we become aware of the need for love on the part of those who are strangers and enemies to us. It is because we know that when we were distant from Him He abolished the separation between us, that we become concerned for those who are distant from us. Because it is the purpose of Christ to bring the whole of creation to fulfillment in relation to Himself, our purpose as Christians includes our continued participation in Christ's mission to the ends of the earth and to the end of time.

This sense of the unlimited inclusiveness of the mission of the Church is expressed by the young Roman Catholic theologian, Father Gregory Baum, *"The Church that claims to be universal should refuse to define its own boundaries in the world."*

> What are the reasons for this position? The Church was created by what Christ did for us on the cross, and since the people purchased by Christ on the cross was the whole human family, there exists a basic identification between the Church and the humanity into which she is sent. This identification is acknowledged constantly by the Church in her faith and her prayer. Because of the intentional unity between the Church and humanity, the grace of Christ is active everywhere in the world. Even though the means of grace are concentrated in a singular and complete fashion in the visible Church, all of humanity has been touched by the redemptive work of the Lord and His saving grace appeals to the hearts of men everywhere, preparing and initiating the kingdom. As in the Israel of old there was "Church before the Church," so now in the world there is "Church outside the Church." Since the community of the Lord calls her own that part of humanity which has been touched and renewed, however partially, by the redemption of Christ, she will refuse to define her own limits. She will never say: "I only stretch to this line, and you, beyond, don't belong to me."
> Especially in our own day it is of great importance that in announcing the Christian message we do not only declare the separation of the Church from the world of the unredeemed, but that with equal confidence we proclaim the Church to be the *sacrament of humanity*, the divine instrument of a transforming movement that is universal.[5]

If this is true, it is indeed a grave danger for the Church to allow itself to think in terms of self-salvation and defense. This would be to raise the walls of partition, not to break them down, to sharpen the boundaries that separate men from one another and from God, not to cross them. We must resist every temptation to retreat into a narrow pietism, the character of which gradually becomes more restricted and self-defeating, until the Church everywhere is fighting only a rear guard action, with outmoded weapons, on fronts already by-passed by the major forces engaged at this moment in history.

It is a curious paradox that just as the era of missions is coming to an end, the world-wide nature of the mission of the Church is coming into clearer focus. The mission of the Church is to be present "as the sacrament of humanity" wherever man is present, and especially at those points on the globe or in the midst of each society where oppressive and de-humanizing forces are most clearly at work. There is no need to list them here. Many are described in other chapters. In discerning missionary priorities, therefore, we must be guided not only by such census information as the fact that there is only one clergyman for every million persons in West China, but also by information, readily available, concerning the sociological, economic, and political problems faced by humanity on almost a world-wide scale today.

Bishop Stephen Bayne speaks of the emergence of one world culture, urban culture. Is not the very existence of the slums of Calcutta at least as clear a Macedonian call as a formal invitation from the National Christian Council of India? And yet we are no more successful than the churches of Asia and Africa in relating the Christian gospel to industrial culture, to secular man in mass society. The new tasks cry out to be undertaken, not in isolation from one another, but on a world scale, aware of the implications of what may be learned in one country for the mission of the Church in other places, in one church for other churches. Are we prepared to see a "foreign missionary" sent out by our church today simply to *learn* from a Kagawa in Japan, or a Chinese social worker in Hong Kong? Is it clear to us why it is important for the Church to be present, even without plan or program, in the midst of suffering and turmoil in Algeria or the Gaza Strip—a tiny community of perhaps three or four persons, without solutions to offer, without the possibility of direct evangelism, but really there, keeping with their whole lives the vigil of God? If this may be true for such missionaries today, it may also be true for the Church everywhere; to the extent that we are conscious of our engagement with universal issues, we may be effectively involved in the Church's world-wide mission.

The interdependence of a rapidly changing, mobile, mass communications world means that we hinder one another almost as much as we help. The world-wide mission of the Church stands also as judgment upon what the Church actually is and does—one might say "at all times and in all places"—for the newer churches are as much subject to the judgment of God as the older and stronger ones. Foreign missions, in some form, *must* continue, to prevent us from falling into the worship of merely tribal gods. Today the selfish, private decisions of local congregations on race relations, building programs, or stewardship, have a direct and sometimes immediately visible effect on the life and mission of native churches in Asia and Africa.

The decisions of American Christians in the "secular" issues of economic aid to developing countries, immigration, or the support of the United Nations, involve them, whether they believe in missions or not, in Christ's ministry to the world. The political decisions of Christians in Africa or China or Korea affect not only the life of their own nations, but our lives and the peace of the globe. We are vulnerable to one another as never before, we need each other as never before, and we face the same secular challenges to Christian faith, and the same demands for radical transformation of the forms of Church life and the structures of missionary outreach.

Is it possible, then, to formulate a new missionary strategy on a global and ecumenical scale? After some years of observing and participating in various attempts to do so, the writer has grave doubts whether it can ever be done. The Olympian approach was appropriate, if it ever was, only to an earlier age of unquestioned Western supremacy and unexamined paternalism. Despite the common description of the problems and opportunities facing the Church on every continent, or because of that fact, the determination of goals, the allocation of resources, and the recruitment of leadership can only be determined by common study and mutual agreement among churches and missionary agencies in each situation. In each regional, national, or local situation, social change is occurring at a different pace; different types of human needs seem to be of paramount importance; local resources are available in differing kinds and degree.[6] If it is difficult to plan a grand strategy for the whole world from some central headquarters, what *can* happen is that each congregation and each denomination can review its own work at home in the light of the total task of the world Church!

Recently, under the auspices of the East Asia Christian Conference, representatives of churches and mission boards with work in Asia met in a series of "Situation Conferences," in a regional attempt to reach a common mind concerning the particular tasks to which God was calling them in their situation at this moment in history. A series of questions was sent out to each of the churches in advance. It must have been a novel experience for many of them, used to dealing only with some Western church headquarters, to be requested by their fellow Christians in Asia, who in many cases represent rival denominations, to evaluate their present work and plans for the future. Some of the questions which Asian Christians saw fit to ask one another, we in the United States would do well to ask ourselves, if we wish to continue, in our situation, to be what we are called to be, a missionary community:

1. What are the positions that must be held at all costs, if we are to continue obedient to Jesus Christ, and if we are to help make him more widely known, and loved, and served?

2. What are the growing edges of the Church's work and witness which must be encouraged and supported?

3. Are there things which the churches have been doing which should now be given up (a) because they are out of date, (b) because they are unproductive, (c) because they are wasteful of resources of time, men, and money?

4. Are there activities of the Church which ought to be handed over to other agencies, and, if so, what are they?

5. What are the new tasks to be undertaken?

6. In what way can the over-all task be thought out and carried out together by the total people of God in each area? [7]

NOTES

[1] Paul Albrecht, *The Churches and Rapid Social Change,* Doubleday and Co., 1961, p. 111.

[2] Christane Rochefort, *Warrior's Rest.*

[3] "The Missionary Implications of the End of Western Colonialism and the Collapse of Western Christendom," *History's Lessons for Tomorrow's Mission,* World Student Christian Federation, Geneva, 1960, p. 196.

[4] Bulletin of Le Centre Protestant d'Etudes et de Documentation, April-May, Geneva, 1960, p. 8.

[5] "Who Belongs to the Church," the *Ecumenist,* Vol. 1, no. 4, 1963, Toronto.

[6] For the important role of "culture focus" in determining response to the Gospel, see M. J. Kerskovits, *Man and His Works,* Alfred Knopf, New York, 1952, especially Chapter 32.

[7] For a fuller statement of these questions and a summary of the answers obtained, see *Reports of Situation Conferences,* published by the East Asia Christian Conference and distributed by the World Council of Churches, New York and Geneva, 1963.

15. Liturgy

DON H. COPELAND

Liturgy can never be a contemporary issue in the Church—for those who regard it in terms of externals, rubrics, ceremonial, formalism and "praying out of a book." It just can't be that important. Before liturgy can be seen to be of great importance, we must travel from a position where it is looked upon as concerned with the environment of one or another style or manner of worshipping God, to the place where liturgy is defined in terms of the nature of Christian worship and its function in God's plan "to reconcile to himself all things, whether in earth or in heaven" (Col. 1:20, RSV). When this journey has been made, then does the liturgy emphatically become momentous, something to be reckoned with.

What is liturgy? Scholars are far from agreed on a definition. Thirty are reviewed by Hermann A. P. Schmidt in "Introductio in Liturgiam Occidentalem." Many acclaim Louis Bouyer's perceptive description where he says:

> Liturgy is to be seen as the meeting of God's People called together in convocation by God's Word through the apostolic ministry, in order that the People consciously united together, may hear God's Word itself in Christ, may adhere to that Word by means of the prayer and praise amid which the Word is proclaimed, and so seal by the Eucharistic sacrifice the Covenant which is accomplished by that same Word.[1]

138

Undoubtedly one of the best definitions of liturgy is that given in the Encyclical Letter, "Mediator Dei," of Pope Pius XII, "The sacred liturgy is the public worship which our Redeemer, the Head of the Church, renders to the Heavenly Father, and which the society of Christ's faithful renders to its Founder and through Him, to the eternal Father. Briefly, liturgy is the public worship of the Mystical Body of Christ, of its Head and of its members."

"Head and members." Here we find a clue to the passionate regard so many have for the liturgy. Here lies our point of encounter with the God of history. Sacred history is the story of God's intervention in the world to draw men to Him, to communicate His divine life to them, and thus to bring about His universal reign. In Dom Cyprian Vagaggini's penetrating insight, "Liturgy is the means of our insertion into that history." Since

> the liturgy includes not only an attitude and an activity of the Church towards God, but also an attitude and an activity of God towards the Church, . . . the liturgy is not a monolog of the Church thinking of God and honoring Him; it is a dialog between God and the Church, a point of contact and a place of meeting. In the liturgy there is both the sanctification of the Church of God and the worship rendered to God by the Church. And since this double action is realized only through Christ and in Him, one may say that the liturgy is the point of encounter, in Christ, of God who sanctifies the Church and the Church who renders her worship to God.[2]

Now we can begin to see some of the reasons for the worldwide concern for liturgical renewal that is sweeping across all the historical divisions of Christendom, and, in the process, becoming a potent force for drawing the separated fragments closer to one another. Liturgy is our point of encounter with God, in the stream of salvation-history, in Scripture, in sacrament, as human beings created by God in the space-time continuum; the point of encounter of God, who sanctifies the Church, and of the Church, who renders her worship to God.

This encounter is by, in, and through Christ Jesus our Lord, made possible by our incorporation into Him through Holy Baptism. Therefore we worship as the Church. Our worship is the Church's worship. When the Church assembles for the offering of her liturgical worship in any place, we have a worshipping congregation, not a congregation of worshippers. What is done in worship is done together, as a unit, as a family, as one body, as the Church, however little the individual members may be aware of this.

Awareness comes to life with catechesis, with reflection upon the liturgical Scriptures, with participation. This in turn has its fruit in Christian formation, in Christlikeness, in attaining "to the measure of the stature of the fullness of Christ" (Eph. 4:13, RSV).

Three months after his elevation to the pontificate, on the Feast of St. Cecilia, 1903, Pius X issued a *motu proprio* ("on his own impulse," a letter by the Pope which has been written on his personal initiative and bears his personal signature). This letter dealt with needed reforms of musical standards, and the restoration of Gregorian chant to its rightful place in the Church. In that document St. Pius wrote a sentence that has become a classic and seminal statement concerning the liturgy. "The primary and indispensable source (fount) of t᾿ ᷓ true Christian spirit is active participation in the solemn mysteries and in the public prayers of the Church."

Liturgy is a noble word. It concerns people. It is the work of the People of God. It is the work of the People of God engaged in the highest activity of which they are capable. It signifies the Christian action, the engagement to which "a chosen race, a royal priesthood, a holy nation, God's own people" (I Pet. 2:9), the One, Holy, Catholic and Apostolic Church is called.

Liturgy concerns people because it is essential to their Christian formation—their new birth, growth, education, and maturity as members of Christ's Body. The worship of Almighty God is the supreme activity to which men are called. "Man is made to praise, reverence and serve the Lord his God and by this means to save his soul" (St. Ignatius Loyola). "Man's chief and highest end is to glorify God and fully to enjoy him forever" (Westminster Catechism).

Liturgy proclaims the salvation history of the People of God, making real the Paschal Mystery whereby the Christian re-lives with Christ that mystery, and keeps the Christian oriented towards God, thus saving him from the idolatry of self.

What was the primary agency wherewith the Church turned the world upside down and converted the Roman Empire if not her liturgical worship? For fifteen hundred years the Lord's Day was regarded by all Christian people as the day for a plenary meeting of the Christian community. The Sunday Eucharist was the occasion at which the Church became visible precisely as a Church. Until the time of Gregory the Great, Sunday was basically nothing other than that. It was the most important, usually the only pastoral activity of those days.

Jungmann reminds us that in Christian antiquity there were no Christian schools of any kind. Until the fourth century at the earliest, whatever organized schooling there was to be found was in the hands of pagans. There were no catechism classes. Children had to be taught Christian doctrine and life by their parents. The Church had no departments of Christian Social Relations, of Christian Education or Finance, no organized youth movement, no missionary societies, no devotional guilds or confraternities. The one and only Christian association was the Church herself. The only meeting was on Sunday, and on Sunday the Church assembled for the liturgy, a living liturgy that was closely connected with the life and feeling of the people. It was an action in which the whole Christian family participated, each one in his degree and order, fulfilling his part, re-living the Mystery of Christ and in the process being transformed by it. Jungmann says:

> The very period of history in which all the above features were missing was the period in which Christianity triumphed over paganism . . . not only exteriorly but also interiorly . . . it was the period in which was effected a complete revolution in contemporary thought by a new

evaluation of human life, of the position of women, of slaves and of
children in human society. . . . When we look for visible and human
factors to which we can ascribe this amazing transformation, we can
find none other than the liturgy of the Church, especially the Sunday
mass-liturgy. . . . We of the twentieth century are in a paganized
world, in a secularised atmosphere which . . . has penetrated into
the midst of our people and has largely de-christianised them. We
are not in so strong a position that we can afford to neglect the great
power which could be derived from a living Sunday liturgy suited to
the people. It is for all who have the care of souls to make the most
effective use of those possibilities which are now at our disposal, and
to work with them for the building up of the Church and the Christian renewal of the world.[3]

Liturgy is therefore intensely pastoral. Its aim is that of leading the faithful to form a closely knit union in the Body of which
Christ is the Head, and to participate according to their station
in that worship that is the worship of the whole Church of
Christ, to the end that all the members of the Body *live truly
the life of Christ*. Although the revival of interest in liturgy and
the beginnings of the liturgical movement are often said to have
sprung from romantic sources, in the twentieth century it has
taken its true direction and is seen in proper perspective—at
once, biblical, sacramental, and pastoral. Because liturgy is so
vitally a pastoral matter, it is (or ought to be) a primary concern
of the chief pastors—the bishops—and of parish clergy, the men
who are responsible under God for the spiritual growth and welfare of the souls committed to their charge.

In the Roman Church the liturgical movement has become a
pastoral-liturgical apostolate that is the pulse-beat of that
Church's work for the salvation of souls and the implementation
of its obedience to the divine commission.

In the Anglican Communion and Lutheran churches there
are stirrings that clearly indicate that the importance of pastoral
liturgy is coming to the front. Liturgical renewal in the Anglican
Communion began with the reforms in the Church of England
in the sixteenth century. For reasons too well known to be repeated, much of this was aborted. The altar and Eucharist lost
their centrality, thus drying up one principle source of spiritual

vitality. People surrendered their participation to choirs and clergy. There was as much non-participation and non-involvement as there was in the Latin Church, in spite of the use of the vernacular language. Too many meaningful signs and symbols were surrendered. Holy Week ceased to be a re-living of the Paschal Mystery. Above all the people were not taught the deepest meanings of their Faith. Lamentably, this is still too true! Recent statistical studies have confirmed suspicions of the indifference and casualness of Episcopalians towards their Christian duty "to worship God every Sunday in his Church." Voices in places high and low frankly deplore the religious illiteracy of Episcopalians. What Dom Gabriel M. Braso has written with contemporary Spanish culture in mind could stand almost word for word as an indictment of Anglican religious education:

> We can state that the cause, or the causes, of the great separation between the Christian people and the Church's liturgy are: lack of faith and lack of religious instruction; or, if you will, lack of faith through lack of religious instruction. If we examine other points of the practical Christian life in our times, we arrive always at the same conclusion; our people are suffering from a very grave evil, ignorance. This is behind their lack of faith, their dechristianized mentality, the superficiality of their life. It accounts for their inability to understand the liturgy, as also for the existence of so many problems in the field of morality that are insoluble. The profound, positive principles of the Christian mystery, the value and meaning of the Church's public worship are unknown. There is no understanding of the eminently positive aspect of the gospel morality or of the extent of its practical requirements, which must shape the Christian's life from its very roots.[4]

Today, however, there are some hopeful signs that these weaknesses are acknowledged and efforts made to correct them.

A Roman Catholic priest-scholar and friend said to me, "I have often felt that were men of different traditions able to get together more often, they would receive inestimable insights into even the ins and outs of their own tradition. How often our own particular problems of a liturgical nature would see an earlier solution if we had close at hand the valuable experience of so many others actively and interestedly engaged in the same field of studies and apostolate!" Is each church to go off on its own tangent, posing thereby a serious threat to the unity of the churches of this great international segment of Christendom? It is the hope of some that the World Center for Liturgical Studies (at this writing in process of development) may provide the resources and setting whereby liturgical scholars can meet and grapple with this problem.

The worship that man owes to God, first by reason of his creaturehood, and second by reason of his redemption, is not a nebulous thing, vague and ill-defined, but is an action of the whole man, personality, body-soul, with content, substance and plan. The plan of our worship is given by Jesus Christ and developed by Him, i.e., by the Church which is His Body, through the direction of the Holy Spirit. I have seen no better theological statement of this than that given by Dom Gabriel Braso:

> There is a glory that is necessary to the perfection of the divine being
> . . . This essential and most perfect glory God expresses in an eternal
> and substantial Word: His Word, His Son, "the brightness of His
> glory and the image of His substance" (Heb. 1:3). Here, then, is
> God's plan: the Word will unite with a human nature, and the human
> family will thereby be introduced into the divine family. As He will
> be Son of God and Son of Man also, all men will share divine sonship
> in Him. At the same time, having the Son of God in their midst, they
> will possess Him who is the splendor and the manifestation of the
> Father's glory. He Himself, being appointed high Priest of mankind,
> will be able to present Himself to the Father as mankind's tribute of
> glory; and men, united in a vital way with Jesus Christ in the unity of
> one mystical Body, will be able to unite their worshipful acts to the
> sacrifice of Jesus Christ. Thus they will cooperate with Him in the
> formation of a single worship, the worship of the Christian religion.[5]

NOTES

[1] Louis Bouyer, Liturgical Piety, University of Notre Dame Press, 1954, p. 39.
[2] Cyprian Vagaggini, O.S.B., Theological Dimensions of the Liturgy, Liturgical Press, Collegeville, Minn., 1959, p. 18.
[3] Joseph A. Jungmann, S.J., The Sacrifice of the Church, Liturgical Press, 1956.
[4] Gabriel M. Braso, O.S.B., Liturgy and Spirituality, Liturgical Press, 1960, p. 210.
[5] Ibid., p. 64.

16. Layman and Priest: The Ministry of the Whole People of God

LAYTON P. ZIMMER

"Grant that *he* may have power and strength to have victory, and to triumph, against the devil, the world, and the flesh. *Amen*" (*Book of Common Prayer*, p. 278).

That variable pronoun, "*he*," in the third supplication in the Ministration of Holy Baptism refers specifically to each and all of us, layman and priest; to you and me. The calling—the ministry—is *ours*. But laity and clergy see their calling in different ways.

The problem is, simply, that a wide gap has long since grown between the generally accepted understanding of the nature and function, respectively, of layman and priest in God's ministry in the world. The laity are widely understood to be receivers of something "good" dispensed only by the clergy in church; a militia called together for a short time one day a week and then sent back to civilian life. They tend to be spectators of whatever struggle of word or deed there may be between their ordained ministers and the world. The clergy, on the other hand, have come to be regarded as the only trained and licensed fighters in the theological-spiritual ring. At the same time, they are seen as beasts of burden bearing the active responsibilities of all

145

the people of God. They are priests, pastors, prophets, administrators, teachers, therapists, civic leaders, witnesses for Christ, social lions, public pray-ers, speech-makers; the list of roles the clergy must attempt to fill, however inadequately, seems endless.

Because of these differing concepts, the life and work of the Church is compromised and confused. Laymen can avoid the pain and challenge of crucial issues; they are spared the turmoil and burden of active responsibility for the ministry; and the clergy grow closer to complacency or despair, depending upon their personal reaction to their god-like role.

The Body of Christ, broken and pierced in so many ways, is seriously hurt by the separation between layman and priest. The healing of this separation is part and parcel of the valid binding up of all the other divisions. We deny the Gospel and scandalize our calling when we differentiate between churches, classes, races or nations—and when we differentiate between the obligation to Christ owed by priest apart from the laity.

Not only are we one in the sight of God, we are one in our responsibility to Him. We are one in our relationship with Him and in our need for Him. We share in each other's plight, if you will; and in our common commitment we likewise share in God's calling to be used in reaching out to all others. Like commitment means like responsibility.

This is not to say that there are no differences in the means of ministry open to, say, a shop clerk vis-à-vis a priest. Certainly, there are real differences; but they are details of function, not fundamentals of nature nor of the overall goals of their Christian calling. Each ministers to each other and, with the other, to all others.

A priest's celebration of the Eucharist, his dispensing of the sacraments, his pastoral care, and his preaching are all parts of his ministry to his congregation. So is the witness of his life in the total experience of the community. Similarly, the congregation's prayers and offerings for the needs of themselves and others everywhere are parts of its ministry. More to the point, though, the witness of the life of each of the souls in that congregation, including the priest's, is the ministry of the Church to the world, in the world.

The concept of ministry *to* anyone by someone else is, by itself, a limited, even sterile idea. It is condescending. The fullness of the Christian ministry is that each of us *with* others grapples with "the devil, the world, and the flesh."

In some parishes, we are beginning to see small groups of laypeople who have committed themselves to assisting in services and to making calls on newcomers, sick folk and shut-ins. Such laymen invariably come to exercise great influence in the life of their parish, not through office or power but through witness and example. They soon begin to take an increasingly conscientious burden on themselves to reflect their convictions of Christ in their given vocations. In the deepest terms of ministry, these people become a pool of concern, response, and imaginative action—a real Faithful Remnant in the life of the Christian community. The sum of their individual abilities is far greater than that of any individual priest or of the professional staff of most parishes, for that matter. They "minister" in their own God-given ways and their ministries are as unique and meaningful as that of any ordained clergyman. In concert with the work of their priests, such laymen widen the horizons of parish life almost beyond belief—or, at least, almost to Gospel standards.

Most active clergymen have heard these terrible and true words more than once: "But you just can't understand!" or, "You don't know what it's like!" or, "Oh you've never been through anything like this." The plain fact is that no man has experienced everything. No man could or should. In the broadest understanding of ministry, though, there are those who have suffered, who do know, who can identify and help in a way some others of us can't. This is the great joy and glory of a fully exercised ministry of the whole people of God.

We have all known those ill or grieved who have been touched by the constant, careful ministry of neighbors far more deeply and meaningfully than by the best efforts of their priest. Priestly

concern and support is tremendously important, of course. The
prayers and sacraments of the Church are basic to the understanding of and growth through pain. But the minute-to-minute
care, the revealed, incarnate love of family, and neighbors, and
friends gives life in the context of ministry and sacraments, as a
parish priest can only rarely hope to do through his own time,
abilities, and personality.

Think how a crippled practical nurse would minister to a
patient who has lost a limb through surgical amputation. Note
how more and more clergy are bringing businessmen, parents,
concerned parishioners, or thoughtful housewives together to
talk to each other, not to listen to ministerial observations and
homilies. Watch the changes in speech and living that occur in
the member of a social clique when one of their own becomes
convinced of, converted and committed to Christ.

The undeniable impact of lay witness to laity is revolutionary
in its connotations to contemporary churchmen. These laymen
are not paid; they are not in any sense professionals. They say
what they themselves believe; they reflect their convictions in
their lives; they are understandable and acceptable precisely because they are not priests, with the medieval, irrelevant, emotional professionalism that that word commonly implies to so
many laymen.

If the burdens of the ministry are understood to be the responsibility of priests alone, and if the clergy should escape the
ever-present threats of pride or disillusionment that are bred by
this magnifying of their tasks, still the best end for which we
can hope is a thorough pastoral ministry to some, an inadequate
ministry to many, and an increasing number of burned-out
priests. Also, the opportunity for real growth amongst the laity
will have been missed by just the degree that they have not
been able to share in the ministry.

Apart from the more pastoral aspects of the ministry, the
Church today is growing in its understanding of the layman's
calling to ever greater involvement in and leadership of the
worship of the congregation. Layreaders are being developed and

used as never before; not just in the absence of a priest (which
so often also means in the absence of many people who won't
worship without a "real minister to put on the service"), but
regularly in well-staffed parishes. Such men read lessons in Morning and Evening Prayer and the Epistle in celebrations of the
Eucharist. They sometimes lead the congregation in the col-
lects and prayers.

Two things grow out of such lay participation in the leading
of worship. First, the layreaders themselves quickly become concerned with the whole of every service. They develop new interest in and literate command of many more facets of liturgical
understanding than they would otherwise; and they share this
with their friends, espccially with those in the parish. The
worship life of a congregation can be transformed by the witness
of several such men.

There is a parish grappling with a wonderful problem right
now that grows out of just this type of experience. Several layreaders there decided that the Epistles are largely unintelligible
when read aloud in service without any opportunity for inter-
lineal exposition. On their own initiative they bent some rubrics
and read the text of the Epistle from the New English Bible at
several successive eleven o'clock Sunday celebrations of the Eucharist. When the rector caught up with this erroneous practice
and stopped it, he was thrilled to find that the congregation had
noticed the change immediately and, in many cases, actively
resented the return to the lovely, archaic confusion of the Prayer
Book translation. Thanks to the layreaders, that parish will wait
impatiently for the revision of the Prayer Book with a deepening
understanding of why it is necessary.

The second fruit of regular lay involvement in the actual
leadership of worship in a parish is that the layreaders themselves grow in their utilization of an increasing number of the
opportunities to worship that exist, but are now so largely un-
used. We hear of more family prayer, more thoughtfully graced
meals, more individual and group Bible study and mcditation.
Such laymcn have even organized and carried on the regular

saying of the evening office in the parish church, complementing the clergyman's daily reading of Morning Prayer.

Here again, in our life of worship, there is a clear calling to the laity to minister with their priests.

There is no doubt that every man ordained to the priesthood of the Church is in constant need of ministry to himself as he seeks to carry on his own ministry to his people. This, too, is an area in which the ministry of laymen must be developed. There is so little understanding of this aspect of mutual commitment and responsibility that many congregations are stunned when their priest suddenly decides to look for a call elsewhere, or when he breaks down (in the performance of his duties, in his personal behaviour, or in his mind or spirit), or when he physically collapses and perhaps dies. Clergy are often lonely, often despairing, especially in this time of religious institutionalism and culture-seduction of the churches.

No matter how fine a pastor the bishop may be, no matter how warm the relationships between one parish priest and several of his neighboring brethren, there is no substitute for those concerned, stalwart parishioners who care for him as a person and will listen to—and talk honestly to—their lonely shepherd. After all, analogies do break down at some point; and Christian people must be expected to think, to speak, to listen, and to care for others considerably more than can real sheep.

This facet of the lay ministry is crucial enough, simply in terms of the needs of the clergy. More than this, though, the whole life of a parish benefits when its clergy are able to keep in close, sympathetic touch with the thoughts and feelings of its people, and when they are able to stay close to their priest, supporting, challenging, criticizing, loving.

It may sound as if this were an almost automatic relationship that is built into every parish set-up, but it isn't. People are people, and so are clergy; and this being true, the difficulties of non-communication always threaten. Too often, they close in and overwhelm.

It is my profound conviction that the life of the Church will not again be a vital, Christly entity in the life of our age and culture until the laity are free to bear Christ's cross—and His image—in the world themselves, in all the myriad ways open only to them by virtue of their non-priestliness. The laymen are the servants of the Lord who have the real money and power of this world, as well as its fear, pain, and confusion. They are the soldiers of Christ who, in their vocational variety, comprise a splendidly trained and equipped army that awaits only challenge and opportunity.

The faithful mind boggles at the thought of what would happen if, say, seventy per cent of all baptized Christians became active, regular worshippers of Christ; or if half the families in each parish would read, pray, and discuss the Faith in their own homes; or if all the good people now enmeshed in pleasantly busy committee or guild work in the institutional Church would give their time and talents and treasure to personal ministry and open witness for Christ in the face of the factual evils and ills of our world. Yet all these resources and fruits of the Gospel will seem unreal or impossible, until the calling of all Christians to the ministry of the whole people of God is promulgated and developed in the Church.

A priest-centered church is dead, although its outward façade may be lovely and impressive indeed. Our Lord knew this, and declared it with clarity and power. God grant that we may hear and understand.

17. Theology in the Space Age

MYRON B. BLOY, JR.

Recent headlines in *The New York Times* proclaimed:
"MISSILE MAKERS TURNING TO SPACE, Industry Is in
the Midst of Sweeping Changes in Production Pattern, Controversy Likely, Research and Development Spending to Soar—
Rise in Competition." [1] The article which follows describes, in
financial and production figures, the change of government research and development priorities in the last ten years from
aircraft to missiles and now to space. Washington financed research and development in space projects now costs $15,500,-
000,000 yearly and is occupying increasing numbers of scientists
and engineers—at the present time about seventy per cent of the
total number.

A more homely but hardly less profound sign of the times is
visible in the neighborhoods of our country, where children are
seen wearing fishbowl "space helmets" rather than the familiar
two-gun regalia of our Western past; toy shops are loaded with
launching pads, rockets, and other necessary apparatus for space
travel; television heroes increasingly carry on their stunts of
righteous derring-do while rocketing through hyper-space.

No one can doubt that we are entering into an exciting, in-
itially bewildering period in man's history which could be called
"The Space Age," but it is easier to point to the outward signs
of the new age than to describe its significance in our spiritual

152

history. We know that we stand at one of the great turning points of history, but we have not had time to discover very many of its dominant meanings.

Some things are already clear, however. William Carlos Williams once pointed out that in the early days of the American Colonies men were content to huddle on the East Coast of the continent in imitation of English villages, and that Daniel Boone led the way into a new, imaginative orientation for Americans when he turned to the West, discovered the Cumberland Gap, and taught us how to live in terms of our own land. Thus the frontier spirit was born: instead of turning our backs to the frontier, we kept pressing through it, discovering ingenious ways of adapting ourselves to its conditions, finding more glory than fear in the thought of its unknown reaches.

Later, this searching, creative spirit found an outlet in the rough and ready technology necessary for the industrial growth of the nation: unknown answers to productive problems were, like the frontier, challenges to our imagination rather than limits to the possible. Now we have a new frontier, space, which demands a different kind of creativity, namely a technology which is dependent on and able to use the incredibly complex and abstract insights of contemporary science. The courage of Daniel Boone and pragmatic genius of Henry Ford are still necessary to our newest frontier, but our frontiersmen also require a mathematical intelligence, trained for years in an academic setting, which would probably leave both Boone and Ford at the starting gate.

Although Americans have always been suspicious of intellectuals, preferring swash-buckling canniness to calculated intellectualism in its heroes, the egg-head is increasingly coming into his own: like it or not, he is the necessary hero of the space frontier and, adaptable people that we are, we are adjusting ourselves to the change. Thus, although the Space Age in one sense is simply a resurgence of the American frontier spirit, it also represents the emergence of the intellectual technologist as our new folk hero. The man in the white lab coat masterfully manipulating a huge 7090 IBM computor is slowly but surely taking the place of his predecessor in chaps and six-shooters who cleared the West of bad guys.

This new phenomenon challenges Christian theology in three crucial ways. In the first place, since all our former heroes (the frontiersman, the cowboy, the inventor, the industrialist) were rugged individualists, we could understand them in simple, individualistic moral terms; the so-called Christian Virtues, which every man could readily understand and imitate, were the explanation of their success. The power of grace was seen to be individualistically manifested. But our heroes today turn out to be not so much specific persons as somewhat anonymous individuals whose main identity is their vocation. It is the public, collective characteristics of the space technologist which make him a hero and not his private, individualistic feats. Part of the reason for this change is that the new technology is so intellectually esoteric for most of us that we couldn't distinguish between the abilities of technologists even if we tried, but also because any one great feat of space technology so obviously requires the collective efforts of thousands of nameless scientists and engineers. Thus, if Christian theology is to make any sense at all out of the Space Age—if we see anything to affirm in our new heroes—we must find ways of identifying grace collectively as well as individually; we must break loose from our sentimental, private versions of God's activity in history and try to understand the way He works through the *vocation* of technology. (It is, perhaps, not too much to hope that the effort to respond to this challenge will also encourage us to venture more deeply into an understanding of other areas of man's public, collective life.)

However, as Paul Ricoeur points out in a remarkably discerning essay, Christian theology has had little insight into the collective power of grace in secular history:

> Do we know how to seek out the *superabundance* of grace which is God's answer to the *abundance* of Evil? Oh, of course, we know the orthodox answer: the superabundance of Jesus Christ; but what signs

of this do we discern in this vast world? We do not dare to seek out these signs of a superabundance except in the interior experience of an abundant growth in joy, peace and conviction. It is our conviction that sin abounds in the external world, but that grace can superabound only in the interior man. Are there to be no signs of the superabundance of grace except in the interior life or in a few communities living in refuge from the world; no signs of this on the great stage of the world? It must be admitted that, as early as Augustine, the dichotomy was already established; the dominant theological school asserted that sin was perhaps collective, but grace was certainly private and interior.[2]

Our difficulty in discovering the power of grace in collective forms is not really an intellectual problem, but a problem of breaking a bad theological habit which limits our vision of reality. The vision of many Christians is blocked by the expectation that God's power inheres only in the interior lives of Christians; some of us have broken through to see that it also inheres in the interior lives of many non-Christians; but very few of us have developed the expectation of discovering grace in secular, collective forms, and it turns out to be very difficult to *see* what we don't *expect* to see. We must accept the fact that if grace is the power that enables men to grow into that true maturity which is revealed in Jesus Christ, then those collective expressions of our life which encourage us to grow into such maturity are surely bearers of grace. Thus, for example, whenever we see a political institution which encourages the growth of the same wholeness and freedom, the same concern for the neighbor, the same affirmation of life which we see in Jesus Christ, then we can be sure that it is His grace which is empowering that system. Only when we begin to see reality this way are we able to carry out our primary ministry of discovering, celebrating, and nurturing God's gracious power as it moves through the world bringing mankind into its true humanity. Only when we have trained our imaginations to break through our merely parochial expectations so that we are enabled to see the glorious multiformity of God's power—only then will we be open to the possibility of discovering and celebrating and nurturing God's power in that collective enterprise and spirit of technology which is the very stuff of the Space Age.

Even when we have accepted the necessity of our common
ministry based on a wider perception of God's power, we must
also break through our prejudices against the technological spirit
in particular. Most theologians and clergymen are educated ex-
clusively in the liberal arts, have little direct association with the
technological spirit, and thus fall prey to the so-called "two
culture" version of reality which is herewith angrily described by
Vannevar Bush, one of the great engineers of our time:

> It has recently and often been asserted that there are two cultures, and
> that these two cultures are to a considerable extent mutually exclusive,
> and bound to be more so. The first kind is asserted to be scientific,
> involving an understanding of men, their history and emotions. Some-
> times it is implied that the former is crass, narrow, and painfully
> utilitarian, while the second is noble and elevating to the spirit. I wish
> to disagree with the whole absurd bag of tricks.[3]

Dr. Bush goes on to argue with great force that our culture
"cannot be thus fragmented without destroying its inherent
value." Unfortunately, it is difficult to hear a sermon these days
in which science and technology are not patronizingly demeaned
in some off-hand way.

If, however, we bring an unprejudiced appraisal to the technological spirit, we can't help but see manifested in it the gracious power of God in at least two ways. In the first place,
technological advance has enlarged man's freedom of choice:
grinding poverty, incessant work, ubiquitous, debilitating disease,
and life-long hunger pinch man's spirit and narrow his possible
ends to the single issue of survival; but technology, by lessening
such common evils, has opened to the mass of men the possibilities of a larger life where justice, friendship, political freedom,
esthetic enjoyment are real options. We must remember that
without "crass" technology we would be so busy simply trying
to survive that we would have neither the opportunity nor inclination to discuss the crassness of anything! We must also
avoid falling for the silly argument that the value of such freedom depends *absolutely* on how we use it: without realizing and
exercising our freedom of choice, even when we make false
choices, we cannot enter into our true humanity. No one knows

yet what new choices space technology is going to thrust on us, no one knows fully what lies behind our newest frontier, but radical new choices will be presented which will deeply affect mankind for good or ill and we should accept this fact as a holy gift, as a further enlargement of our freedom.

The second way in which technology reveals the grace of God is best described by Lewis Mumford when he says that "no one can hope to achieve any kind of personal integrity in the modern world who is not at home with the machine, who attaches his values only to a pre-machine culture"; he then gives the following definition of the technological spirit:

> This respect for the object, this conscious interest in the actual goal of things, this "functionalism," to use a slang word lately popular in esthetics, is in fact a valuable contribution to the whole personality. Not merely does it exclude irrelevant emotion; but with its sense that the person himself is also an object, to be viewed from the outside by others, it tends toward a certain underemphasis, a certain decent self-effacement, which is in the best style of our epoch.[4]

This functionalism and concomitant humility (which does, in fact, pervade the life of the Massachusetts Institute of Technology where I am Episcopal Chaplain) is clearly a manifestation of the life we see in Jesus Christ and is, thus, a witness to the grace which pervades the collective spirit of technology. Jesus is, of course, clearly a crass functionalist in comparison to the extremely academic stance of the Pharisees. Being and action are never separated in his life: he doesn't talk about health, he heals; he challenges the rich young man to *do* what he says he believes; he tells his disciples that a tree is known by its fruit. And, as you will recall, when John the Baptist sends messengers to find out if he is the "one who is to come," he submits his work to their pragmatic judgment by saying to them, "Go and tell John what you have seen and heard." This impatience with metaphysical hair-splitting, this submission to the given-ness of concrete, eventful reality, and this radical attention to viable results which we see in Jesus Christ is brought to bear on contemporary life by the technological spirit.

Those who can break through a theological narrowness which

has a long history, and who can surmount the prejudice and fear with which most humanists view technology will discover a good measure of God's glory in the accomplishments and spirit of technology. They will thus be enabled to enter into our real ministry in the Space Age: they can rejoice in the freedom-enlarging choices we will be given by space technology and in the tough, yet humble, pragmatic spirit which will inevitably become even more pervasive than it is now. Without this breakthrough, the Church will be condemned to remain in the tight little world of individualistic morality, and the Space Age, with its technological heroes crossing exciting, new frontiers—indeed with its freight of grace—will leave us in a faithless backwash.

The third, and final, point I wish to make is that the ministry of affirmation which I describe is necessarily the burden of laymen. We used to be able to assume that anyone with common sense could apprehend and understand the significant vocational and institutional powers of the day; thus, it could also be assumed that any clergyman could discover how the power of grace was working in any given area of life and nurture its growth. Although it was never *right* to limit this task to the clergyman, now it is *impossible* to do so because only the professionals in the space technology and its allied supportive fields can discern the shape and course that the Space Age is taking. We are all dependent on them. As Professor Joseph Fletcher recently said,

> Our theological education, as it stands today, without the help of theologically-oriented laymen, does not even equip us with knowledge of how to *ask* the questions, to say nothing of finding the answers. *This* is the core of the problem of communicating the Gospel in our times. Theologizing is what takes place where the Gospel intersects with the *world*, and it is laymen—not the clergy—who stand at that point. Constructive theology, as distinguished from systematic, can only get going again with *lay* theologians.[5]

Theologically knowledgeable Christian technologists are the main hope the Church has for creative involvement in the Space Age: they are potentially equipped to affirm and nurture the *true* spirit of technology by constantly judging it from the viewpoint of the spirit of Christ, to see the specific strengths *and* limitations of the technological spirit within the full spirit of Christ and thus to block technology's temptation to prideful fanaticism, and, finally, to lead the rest of us out of our theological parochialism and our suspicion of technology into a creative engagement on our newest frontier—the Space Age.

NOTES

[1] *New York Times*, Sunday, May 5, 1963, Section F, p. 1.
[2] Paul Ricoeur, "The Image of God and the Epic of Man," *Cross Currents*, Winter, 1961, p. 44.
[3] Vannevar Bush, "Two Cultures," *Technology Review*, November, 1962, p. 21.
[4] Lewis Mumford, *Art and Technics*, Columbia University Press, New York, 1960, p. 54.
[5] Joseph Fletcher, "The Professions: A Theological Frontier," *The Friends' News Letter*, July, 1962, published by the Episcopal Theological School in Cambridge, Mass.

18. Education for the Ministry

GIBSON WINTER

There is some consensus today on the difficulties of the ordained ministry in parish and congregation. Interpretations of this phenomenon are diverse, but the significant datum is the experience of pastors.[1] Pastors themselves experience the difficulties largely as frustrations with the administrative task and a general feeling of *the irrelevance both of their ministry and of the church* to any structures beyond the personal needs of some of the congregation. However important such personal concerns may be, there is an increasing sense of distance between the ordained ministers and the life and experience of the contemporary world. The organization provides the only point of contact with the contemporary world, and yet the organization is itself the focus of the alienation between Christian faith and contemporary life.

The general problem of ministry today arises from a breakdown of communication between faith and life, Christ and contemporary culture, Church and world. The ordained ministry is a particularly vulnerable point in this broken communication, since the ministry is the nexus of a Church and world encounter. This is a fundamental datum in reflection on training for the ordained ministry, even as it is the outstanding fact about the missionary task of the churches in the twentieth century.

The center of gravity of education for the ministry is now in theological schools. The American churches have been striving for generations to develop an educated ministry; this general movement coincides with the emergence of an educated society, but it also represents an attempt to move beyond Frontier lay Christianity toward formal, religious institutions and a clerical caste in the churches. The net effect has been the emergence of a seminary-centered training for the ministry over the past one hundred years and the cultivation of the theological disciplines for the trained clergy. This total development undoubtedly has significance for the development of Christian theology and responsibility in American life, but this center of gravity in seminary training has been achieved at the very moment when the prerequisites for such a seminary-centered process of education have come into radical question.

PREREQUISITES FOR SEMINARY-CENTERED TRAINING

Four prerequisites of a seminary-centered training have come into question during the last fifty years.[2] We could do what we are doing in our theological schools, only do it somewhat better, and contribute to the communication of the message and life of the faith rather than aggravating its disruption, if we could assume at least one of these prerequisites.

The four prerequisites of seminary-centered preparation are: 1) viable religious structures; 2) a style of Christian life; 3) a systematic theological perspective; 4) independent persons. There may well be other considerations to which weight should be given, but these prerequisites form the major presuppositions of seminary-centered training.

The Viability of Religious Structures

Much has been said and written about the crisis of *religious institutions* in the contemporary world. This institutional crisis undermines a seminary-centered theological training. Where the religious structures *participate* in the contemporary society, they are *accommodated* to the point of almost total assimilation to the American way of life. This is the burden of Will Herberg's thesis and it has not been refuted at any serious point. Furthermore, where religious structures offer some dimension of transcendence of the culture, some perspective and direction, they are insulated from contact with the structures of the Church and become marginal to the religious enterprise. The tenuous hold of inner-city missions, experimental ministries, industrial efforts and lay academies which attempt more than pietistic retreat, bears ample testimony to this ecclesiastical paradox—the paradox of increasing prosperity of religious organizations of dubious authenticity, and the dissolution of the fabric of religious missions which bear unmistakable marks of courageous witness. Projects like the East Harlem Protestant Parish and the Detroit Industrial Mission do, indeed, elicit support, but their very existence is significant of the institutional dilemma—ministry occurs more and more outside established lines. Projects such as these are actually supported either through endowments of institutions which are converted to new purposes (for example, Judson Memorial) or through the agency of creative leaders who are protected by middle echelons in the denominational enterprise.

When we consider questions of remedy, we constantly confront those who urge a development of *koinonia* in the organization church, or deepened theological work with laity, or refinements in cultus. Whatever our reactions to such suggestions, and the burden of historical proof is certainly increasing for the proponents of such religious renewal apart from renewal of the contemporary world, the institutional crisis subverts seminary-centered theological education. If the religious institutions existed in a viable relationship with the contemporary culture so that worship, preaching and teaching, as well as the *koinonia* of a disciplined community, could serve as structures for proclamation and servanthood, then the seminaries could train men thoroughly in the rationale and contents of such proclamation with a fair presumption that that training would find vehicles adequate to its expression. A seminary-centered education could face difficulties or conflicts in these structures, if the institutions were interwoven with the contemporary world so that they provided viable structures of ministry. However unstable the style of Christian life and the theological perspective, and indeed however limited the independence of the persons, the religious structures would stabilize the work of ministry. Through how many periods of Christian history was this not the case! In periods of theological and spiritual crisis, the institution bore the burden of proclamation and ministry, and informed the culture of the West.

A Style of Christian Life

A style of Christian life could provide continuity for a ministry in the contemporary world. Seminary-centered education could be effective if a style of holiness, an image of sainthood, captured the imagination of contemporary Christians and offered a transparent pattern of life. Such styles of holiness are not usually associated with learned groups or academic institutions in Christian history; indeed movements like the prophetic witness in Israel, medieval lay movements, the Franciscan development, the sects, and other patterns of holiness and witness have generally arisen outside the more cultured structures of the churches. Nevertheless, these movements renewed the mission of the Church; in fact, the monastic movements carried the enormous missionary enterprise in Western Europe; their style of life made a deep impress upon the tribal life of medieval Europe.

In pointing to the absence of any such renewing style in our time, we still acknowledge this possibility as a path through which ministry and renewal may develop.[3] Certainly, the Community of Taizé in France is an example of the possibility of medieval patterns of holiness in the contemporary world of Europe. To what extent Taizé plays on European nostalgia for a lost Christendom is another question. Despite their saintly witness, one must raise questions about their style on the American scene. Certainly the puritanical style of law and restraint no longer holds much appeal in American life. The meaning of the holy, the transparency of contemporary patterns of saintliness, even the *possibility of religious experience* are radically in question today; indeed, laymen give top priority to the congeniality of the clergy, relegating professional competence and quality of life to a minor position. There is no style of holiness through which ministry is now authenticated and recognized. A "calling" is either an institutional formula or a ritual expression. "Personal friend," even "professional friend," characterize the love and holiness of our day; this is rather a sign of our communal crisis than recognition of the holy in the twentieth century.

A Systematic Theological Perspective

The crucial presupposition of seminary-centered training for the ministry is the existence of a biblical foundation for the Message and a coherent formulation of that Message in which preaching and teaching can be grounded. The great appeal of Karl Barth's evangelical theology in the modern world is the hope that it can overcome the problems raised by biblical criticism and provide a theological orientation through which the Message can be proclaimed, and not merely tossed like a stone.

A somewhat modified expression of this same line emerged in biblical theology, which attempted to express the Message implicit in the Scriptures without imposing on the biblical materials an alien philosophical or systematic theology. Although both evangelical theology and biblical theology draw adherents today, both movements failed to deal with the historical critique of the Scriptures and the role of human reason and language in the appropriation of the Scriptural testimony. They attempted to by-pass the crisis in hermeneutics. Nothing even approaching a theological consensus has emerged. The theological world is caught in the deepest kind of crisis and difficulty—a crisis which has thus far been largely concealed from the laity through silence in the churches and preoccupation with organizational activities. In Roger Hazelton's words, "The day of impressive conceptual constructions and dogmatic summations is now past." [4]

The breakdown of communication between theology and the contemporary world is almost total; moreover, this is a breakdown where there is no offense because the proclamation simply does not penetrate in language and forms which can be apprehended. Preaching draws "a blank." Contemporary preaching and teaching are much more pathetic than the trip by a sectarian group to Japan some years ago; firmly convinced that they would be given the gift of speech in every language, the sect group arrived in Tokyo and spoke in gibberish to the puzzled Japanese who listened in idle curiosity and then went about their business. The solution of this theological crisis is critical to education for the ministry. The theological schools are in no position to train for the ministry without recognition of the lack of a coherent theological structure with which to prepare men for the task of proclamation.

The abortive attempts to deal with scientific humanism through biblical theology are nowhere better illustrated than in the collapse of Christian social ethics. The Church's social ethic is a sensitive barometer to the Church-world situation, because social ethics draws its power from theological perspective; moreover, it expresses that perspective in patterns through which life in the world can be sustained and saved. Evangelical theology produces no social ethic because it passes above all of the problems of contemporary anthropology which must be solved before a social ethic can emerge. Indeed, the most significant contribution to a Christian social ethic today is the work of the late H. Richard Niebuhr, but his reflections on the situation generate a contextualist ethic. This may well be the proper direction for our ethical reflection, in view of the theological crisis, but it poses the most serious problems for a seminary-centered education. Reflection on the situation presumes a work of theological reflection that is intimately involved in the situation—not isolated in the halls of academe. The theological school is quite divorced from that context, and the more so today because its reflective work on the Christian Message is disengaged from the existential struggle of an industrial society. The very strength of the theological school for the task of reflection proves to be its greatest weakness in preparation for the ministry, since it has to presume a contextualist disclosure of the meaning of life and yet develops its theological structures apart from that context.

To say this is not to suggest that theological reflection should be ignored or dropped as the crucial focus of theological training. Clearly the task of theological reflection and development of a theological ethic in which the biblical foundations and the contemporary culture come into serious dialogue become much more crucial in our time. Nevertheless, training for the ministry cannot assume that this task is done; rather it engages the student in this task as the lifelong process of his ministry. A seminary-centered education presupposes some framework which can be appropriated and then serve as a perspective from which further theological reflection can develop in the ministry. Such a framework is yet to be formed for our world, and therefore the seminary has to forge a dialogue between its foundations and the contemporary world, in which the student can participate. *This dialogue, rather than a defined theological framework, becomes the context of theological training.*

Preparation of men in the contours of faith and the shape of a Christian society can only be done in a dialogue which crosses the gap of broken communication between Christian foundations and the contemporary world.[5]

Personnel Training for the Ministry

Despite the institutional and theological crisis, a seminary-centered preparation for the ministry could succeed with men who operated independently with a clear sense of calling. In our own time, Cimade has demonstrated the possibilities inherent in the cultivation of a committed group of inner-directed individuals; in fact, the experimental ministries and outstanding congregational ministries of our own time have been created by men of this type. No system can completely inhibit the creative developments which such men can generate, although some eras and some frameworks can encourage rather than hinder

their contributions. A minority church could attract and cultivate this kind of leadership, much as the Reformed Church in
France has developed its own leadership. However, this is not a
live option for our theological schools and seminaries.

The facts characterize the generality of men entering the
ministry today: they are "seeking" rather than "called"; they are
conformist rather than independent. These facts raise real questions about seminary-centered training. A large proportion of the
men training for the ordained ministry are ignorant of the faith,
uncertain of their vocation and seeking their own place within
the Christian faith. This may always have been true in theological schools and monasteries. That observation is quite beside the
point, since the real issue is that such men are not the materials
of an elite corps. Moreover, the modal type of man in seminary,
to use James Dittes' [6] way of stating this, tends to be oriented
to stable, institutional structures and will move toward conformity rather than independent action. These are competent,
decent men who will be able to make real contributions, but
they cannot be trained as an elite in anticipation that they will
operate independently. If they are trained in isolation from these
ambiguous situations with a particular equipment and expertise,
they will make what accommodations are demanded and try to
fulfill the expectations of those around them. This is, at least,
what can be generally anticipated from a seminary-centered approach in the present context with the type of men now entering the ministry. Moreover, there is no reason to assume that the
type of men entering the ministry will or should change; certainly no change can be anticipated apart from the emergence of
a style of holiness that expresses the depth of contemporary
culture or a theological vision which effects communication between the biblical testimony and the structures of contemporary
thought. Indeed, selection for the ministry is undoubtedly interwoven with the other parameters of the ministry of the Church.

There is an inclination to decry the men entering the ministry
or to assume that recruitment of a particular type could change
the situation. We have suggested that a certain type of seminary-

centered training might be viable with a particular type of material, but this would probably be missing the seriousness of the present crisis. Actually much more could be done with and for the men now entering the ministry, if the seminaries engaged with them in the development of theological perspectives and institutional forms through which the Message could be proclaimed and the servanthood of the Church embodied. Their lack of a sense of vocation and a tendency to institutional conformity only reflect the state of the churches through which these men have passed. They are the Church of our day. Theological preparation on the present basis only perpetuates this situation by training the men in a Message and activities which alienate them from the contemporary world, while preparing them for an institutional situation in which their tendencies to conform will be siphoned into organizational activity. Theological preparation fails to take the institutional crisis seriously, but it also divorces theological appropriation from the actual contexts in which it might become a creative force.

We must acknowledge that there are thoughtful men in the churches today who fall back on one or another of these prerequisites as the crucial mode of preparation for the ministry. Some men look to experimental ministries and institutional transformation as the crux of the problem. They see the emergence of missionary forms of Christian life as the basic task and the necessary framework for development of the ministry. The difficulty with making this a monolithic approach is that the men trained for the ministry will undoubtedly be the crucial task force in such a transformation. The present pattern of training subverts this possibility by making every attempt at institutional renewal a threat to the narrow margin of security to which these men cling.

Others look to the deepening of theological reflection as the focus of the contemporary problem. They see the possibility of overcoming the religious crisis by developing theological expertise. This is certainly a possibility for a selected few, but it presumes six or more years of theological training, and it is highly questionable that the present recruits are really fitted for this type of training. Furthermore, a subjectively helpful theological approach is quite a different thing from a ministry of the Church.

Finally, some of the more traditional churches are clinging to a pattern of holiness and worship which they trust to carry their ministry in the midst of theological and institutional ambiguities. Such a solution appeals to the tendencies to institutional conformity among the men entering the ministry, and it also evokes a positive response in the private culture of the residential milieu, since it can be insulated from the real struggle of the contemporary world. In the long run, this priestly culture only deepens the estrangement in the Church-world relationships of our age. Despite our critique of these tempting alternatives through which a seminary-centered preparation for the ministry could be perpetuated, we recognize that sincere Christians firmly believe that one or another of these prerequisites can be re-established without a serious reformation in the theological enterprise. In looking toward a dialogic rather than seminary-centered framework of training for the ministry, we can only be cognizant of those who turn backwards to the cultivation of one of these parameters rather than looking out upon the uncertain terrain of the mission of the Church in this new world.

A DIALOGIC FRAMEWORK OF PREPARATION

Is the seminary or theological school any longer an adequate structure for training the Church's ministry? If not, what substitute would one suggest? A dialogic framework of theological training is a compromise between seminary-centered training and a radically new approach. This compromise is particularly appealing because it draws on the strengths of the disciplined faculties of theological study while bringing their work into the context of the Church's struggle to discern its mission and ministry.

In order to be somewhat more specific, let us consider what would be entailed in the development of a dialogic framework of training for the ministry.

The key to a dialogic framework is objectively meaningful involvement of selected members of the theological faculty in the proclamation and ministry of the Church.[7] Such involvement is missing in occasional lectures and committee activity on the part of faculty members. Most of this activity is "hit-run driving." Moreover, faculty involvement needs to be at crucial points *with the men* whom they are preparing for the ministry, and focussed around the specific role of their own discipline in the mission of the Church. Furthermore, such involvement should not be an extra on top of their theological obligations, but an integral part of their teaching work. *Ministry is the proper context of theological preparation for ministry.* Finally, the development of the Church's ministry cannot be confined any longer to a training of clergy in isolation from laity, so that the objective involvement of faculty will include pastors and laity in the theological work of training. There can and should be, of course, periods of theological work in the quiet of an academic situation, but such reflection becomes integral to training for the ministry when it is set in the larger context of such objective involvement in mission and ministry.

At least two kinds of dialogue are needed for theological education in the contemporary situation: (1) the dialogue of proclamation in contemporary culture and (2) the dialogue of servanthood in the contemporary world. These are two aspects of the same fundamental relationship of faith to culture, but they can be separated as tasks of mission.

The dialogue of proclamation has preoccupied many theologians in our own day, although students preparing for the ministry are seldom creative participants in this dialogue. We tend to think of general theological education as a prerequisite for engaging in such dialogue, and consequently, men are well through their training for the ministry before they even become aware of the dialogue. The notion of general theological education before engagement in this dialogue presumes an academic understanding of theology. Without passing over the serious obstacles presented in our time by the theological ignorance of men entering the seminary, we can still see that theological questions are matters of existence and inextricably involved in every aspect of life and education. The dialogue of proclamation can and should be the framework within which the biblical testimony and historical struggles of the churches are taught. Moreover, theology can best be taught in the framework of contemporary thought—scientific, literary, historical and philosophical. This is the research in which biblical scholars, church historians and theologians are actually engaged. They too often drop this task for the diversionary operation of pumping some distilled content into their students, only to turn back to the real work of reflection in which they are engaged. This latter work of research, set in the context of the Church's apostolate in the world, should be the setting for theological education. The faith and culture dialogue poses the beginning point and continuing frame of reference of theological training. This does not obviate the importance of historical and biblical research in its own right, but that research gains its significance in relation to the Church's apostolate. The implication is that examination of a man who has prepared for the ministry should require the construction of a theological understanding of the Message in relation to some contemporary form of culture—literary, philosophical, historical, or scientific.

The other aspect of dialogue presents special problems for seminary faculties who have little involvement in the struggle to develop a mission in the contemporary world. This dialogue of servanthood can employ certain structures which have been emerging in response to the crisis in the ministry in our day. The development of clinical training can serve as a framework of objective involvement of faculties in personal ministry. The emergence of an urban training center for development of metropolitan mission makes possible an introduction of students and selected faculty to urban contexts. The experience in internship, or "field work," sets a framework for objective involvement of faculty and students in the existing structures of congregational life. Let us consider the implications of this process for the development of curriculum.

The problem with all of the developments in training is that theological faculties tend to shunt their responsibility for training off to these structures. Thus, clinical training becomes a separate experience, divorced from the theological dialogue. The Urban Training Center may well fall heir to a similar divorce. Certainly, internship tends to become simply a way out of the impossible task of training men for an ambiguous ministry in a faculty which is estranged from the problems of ministry. Here the issue of *objective involvement of faculty in a meaningful way* becomes crucial, because the important issues in urban mission, clinical pastoral work, and congregational ministry are the biblical, historical, and theological meanings of these embodiments of the Church's servanthood. Sooner or later we shall have to remove the training for ministry from the theological seminaries unless it becomes possible to establish a dialogic framework between these involvements and the fundamental theological task.

The implications of such dialogue for curriculum would be the establishment of seminars in biblical exegesis, theological reflection, and ethical consideration around three foci of servanthood: mission in an industrial and/or rural setting, clinical pastoral relationships and congregational ministries. These are the contexts in which the dialogue of apostolate can be shaped, but they should include the participation of pastors and laymen from the particular situations. Thus, in the urban context, work in biblical interpretation can be carried on in the settlement house, or, in the industrial context, through the Urban Training Center. Theological reflection with doctors and chaplains can be developed in the clinics, as well as in urban contexts and lay classes in parishes. Training for the ministry is training in apostolate and servanthood. It can no longer be conducted in isolation from that context; in fact, ministry and mission are actually to be developed in the process of training, and this is the joint task of faculty, students, pastors, and laymen. Examination in this aspect of dialogue would involve a biblical and theological interpretation of one of these aspects of ministry.

Theological faculties would participate directly in the Church's missionary task if a dialogic form of training were developed. Such a possibility will fill some faculty with dismay, because they do not wish to be disturbed in their academic pursuits; perhaps, many of these faculty members should be encouraged in these pursuits and included as resource persons in training for the ministry. However, the core faculty who educate for the ministry will enter directly into this critical phase of the Church's contemporary struggle—the discovery of the intellectual and institutional forms of apostolate in our time. Education for ministry will take place in the context of research on the ministry—a context in which pastors and laity will be more than equal collaborators. The total work could be identified as the awakening to consciousness of God's people in the midst of this society.

Such research on the ministry will provide an environment for cultivation of Christian style and personal responsibility. The prerequisites of "seminary-centered" training, now in serious question, can thus be brought into the training process itself.

Renewal of theological training cannot be separated from renewal of mission; thus, the missionary task sets the context of theological training, and the work of apostolate provides the context of theological research.

NOTES

[1] The importance of understanding the pastors' experience was brought out in *The Christian Century* editorial, January 16, 1963, where the editors noted the extensive concern of pastors with difficulties in the ministry—a concern not really shared by administrators, journalists, and seminary professors. The author is indebted to Widick Schroeder's *Religion in American Culture* (to be published), and Thomas C. Campbell's "A Study in the Relation of Theology and Sociology," Ph.D. Dissertation, University of Chicago, 1963, for some of the most accurate data on the experience of ministers and the extent of communication through the ministry.

[2] "Seminary-centered" refers only to institutional context, since within the seminary such education might center upon biblical, theological, philosophical, or psychological studies.

⁵ Gordon Cosby's work at Church of Our Saviour, Washington, D.C., approaches this problem in a serious way, but this could not be done in seminaries detached from society.

⁶ Roger Hazelton, "Ministry as Servanthood," *The Christian Century*, April 24, 1963, p. 524.

⁵ Denys Munby, after many years of work on World Council of Churches commissions, renders a much harsher judgment: "There may be a theology which could be written today to speak to the men of the twentieth century; but it does not seem that our theologians are equipped to write it." (*The Idea of a Secular Society*, Oxford University Press, 1963, p. 83.)

⁶ The author is indebted to James Dittes' remarks on this subject in his mimeographed paper, "What Kinds of Persons Become Ministers?"

⁷ The author is indebted to Robert Lynn's discussion of this type of commitment to the enterprise of ministry in conjunction with critical reflection on the object of commitment; mimeographed paper, "How Can Theological Education Become More Effective?"

PART III

MORALITY IN TRANSITION

19. Peace

ARTHUR E. WALMSLEY

"Peace on earth, which men of every era have most eagerly yearned for, can be firmly established only if the order laid down by God be dutifully observed. The progress of learning and the inventions of technology clearly show that, both in living things and in the forces of nature, an astonishing order reigns, and they also bear witness to the greatness of man, who can understand that order and create suitable instruments to harness those forces of nature and use them to his benefit." [1]

In the opening words of his last great encyclical, *Peace on Earth*, His Holiness, John XXIII, laid bare in Christian terms the dimensions of the dilemma confronting human society today. The technology of war, marked by complex weapons systems of incredible destructiveness, is yet a witness to the ingenuity of man and the orderliness of God's creation discernible to man. Because the forces of nature are open to the greatness of man's understanding, the finding of "suitable instruments" to control technology is possible. Peace can be established, but only if the order laid down by God is dutifully observed.

I

It is significant that the major struggle for "suitable instruments" to control war has been carried on since 1945 not by the

churches, but by governments, scientists, citizens' and professional groups, and increasingly by "peace research" centers. In
1945, shortly after the fateful decision to use the atomic bomb,
a group of nuclear scientists banded together, and their struggles
of conscience led to the excellent "Bulletin of the Atomic Scientists," a monthly devoted to problems of disarmament and arms
control, which in its pages has carried on a lively debate on the
moral issues of war and peace more focussed than any writing
on the subject from a churchly point of view. In the 1950's, a
number of research groups were formed, such as the Rand Corporation and the Institute for Defense Analyses. At first, their
work tended to focus on the planning and development of ever
more complicated weapons systems. More recently, the government has contracted with them, and with various of the elec-
tronics and other firms working on defense contracts, for the
creation of systems of weapons control and detection. At least
fifteen universities have established centers seeking the essential
scientific, economic, political, military, and technical information, and the new formulations needed for a realistic policy for
arms control and disarmament. These centers, such as the Institute of War and Peace Studies at Columbia University, the
Center for Research on Conflict Resolution at the University of
Michigan, the World Rule of Law Center at Duke, and the
Center for Strategic Studies at Georgetown, bring together the
scientific, human relations, and social science communities for
an exploration of the general and specific problems of war and
peace. Their research covers such wide-ranging topics as "alternative ways of handling conflict; behavioral science research towards
peace"; a study of "factors pertinent to the political control of
an international police force"; "techniques for monitoring the
production of strategic delivery vehicles through the entire cycle
from the acquisition of raw materials through the quality testing
of the finished product." [2]

In similar fashion, business and trade groups have held conferences on various aspects of the problems of disarmament. A
variety of professional organizations have held international

meetings, such as the Conferences on Science and World Affairs, and the meetings of a Special Committee on World Peace Through World Law of the American Bar Association. A range of education and action groups have sprung up, some of them committed to the total pacifist position and to tactics of civil disobedience, but the majority, represented by such varying points of view as the United World Federalists, the Foreign Policy Association, the National Committee for a Sane Nuclear Policy, and Turn Toward Peace, committed to making a wide range of alternative policy proposals across the nation.

On September 26, 1961, the United States Arms Control and Disarmament Agency was established by Congress. With a staff of a hundred fifty persons and an annual budget of $6.5 million, it is the one agency of its kind in the world. Growing out of less formalized antecedents (such as the appointment of Mr. Harold Stassen as Special Assistant to the President for Disarmament, in 1955-58), the Agency is a consultative and advisory body to the State Department. Two-thirds of its budget is currently being spent on research.

It may, of course, be argued that these multiple activities of government, voluntary agencies, and research centers miss the point. The United States is engaged in a struggle with a power bloc whose record in breaking international agreements is notorious. The search for political and technological instruments for accomplishing disarmament and arms control, and for creating the conditions of international order, desirable as these may seem in long range terms, has been set alongside a policy of nuclear deterrence and arms buildup the likes of which the world has never seen. A budget of $6.5 million for arms control and disarmament is miniscule alongside a defense budget of $50 billion. The fact is that the most hard-headed diplomats and responsible members of the military on our side, and it is reasonable to speculate this to be the case on the part of our adversaries also, recognize that national security and the future of civilization demand an end to the spiraling costs and threats of an arms race. As Roswell Gilpatric, then Deputy Secretary of Defense, pointed out some months back, "We do not have two policies, a deterrent policy and an arms control policy. We have one policy, which is to safeguard our national security." [3] However one may regard either the morality or the ultimate effectiveness of a policy of deterrence, it is important to note that even the military regard national security (and world peace) as ultimately tied to arms control. The technology of war rushes ahead. Slowly, in the years since 1945, a consciousness is dawning that the same technology can produce safeguards which will gradually lessen tensions and create the possibilities of a genuine international accord. How else explain the tenacious efforts of both the United States and the Soviet Union to achieve a nuclear test ban, and take a first step towards reversing the process of escalation to a third world war?

II

If such an analysis as this seems inappropriate as a basis on which to begin a Christian consideration of the issues of war and peace in our day, it must emphatically be stated that in the contemporary world the issues are in fact being argued in such terms as these and not in traditional Christian categories. The most highly developed Christian teaching on war and peace has centered on the natural law ethic of a "just war." Modern nuclear weaponry, and biological and chemical systems even more terrifying, render meaningless any efforts to justify war fought with such weapons. As the Episcopal Church's House of Bishops said in October, 1962:

> It is becoming increasingly evident that all-out modern war cannot protect the world's peoples, that an atomic holocaust cannot serve the purpose that war may once have served as an instrument of political or police action to secure justice and peace, that total war under modern conditions is self-defeating, and that it will utterly fail to secure peace with the enemy or even peace within the borders of the countries waging it.[4]

The efforts of a few theologians to rehabilitate the "just war" theory by restricting its application to "limited wars" such as the actions in Korea or South Vietnam,[5] only reinforce the awareness that traditional categories of Christian ethics fail to comprehend the problems of the nuclear age. In point of fact, the nature of modern war has rendered largely academic the debate within the Church between those who support a just war variant and those who argue a pacifist position. Roland Bainton, in his excellent survey, *Christian Attitudes Toward War and Peace*, suggests the pragmatic basis upon which Christians and others must come to adopt an anti-war position today:

> At the present juncture there is more need for peace than there is for pacifism. If peace is preserved it will be through the efforts not of pacifists, but of peace-minded non-pacifists, who do not renounce war absolutely, but who oppose war in our time on grounds of the humanitarian and the pragmatic.[6]

Pacifists will disagree with the latter statement at the same time they welcome the support of a new generation of "nuclear pacifists."

Apart from the encyclical *Peace on Earth*, there has been little newsworthy Christian comment on the peace issue in the nearly twenty years since World War II, and almost no Christian impact on national and international events. A few of the churches do maintain programs in international affairs, but these tend to be peripheral and ineffectual.[7] John Bennett, Dean of Union Theological Seminary, expresses the fear that the failure to be active in the struggle for peace is a sign that the churches have succumbed to a "widespread tendency to assume with fatalism and with an abdication of conscience that military necessity is the ultimate law of life in time of war." "Perhaps," he continues, "the silence comes more from sheer bafflement than from callousness." [8]

This failure is not unrelated to problems faced by the Church in ministering in an increasingly complex society. From an institutional standpoint, the churches have had growing difficulty addressing themselves to any of the momentous moral issues of our time. Events move much more rapidly than the structures or the thought forms of the Church. A good case in point is the

crisis in civil rights in the United States. On no single issue has
the official "position" of the churches been as near unanimous.
Yet it was not until the summer of 1963, after repeated crises
forced events to a showdown stage, that institutional patterns
were bent or overridden by some leaders in the churches, who
began to give forceful attention to the issues involved. Whether
such leadership will sustain its momentum is a good question.
Whether such a sense of moral urgency could be generated in
the churches concerning the issues of peace is frankly doubtful.
With respect to peace, no consensus on the issues or on a Christian approach to the issues has been achieved.

                        III

If the churches today cannot give leadership to a quest for
peace, this does not mean that God is not active in leading men
and nations towards peace and a more humane social order. Nor
does it deny the possibility that the churches may recover a moral
seriousness which is today largely lacking. To do this, Christians
must face four problems which. can be drawn out of the fore-
going discussion, problems which are at once intensely theological and intensely practical.

The first is the failure of Christian theology and the organs
of the Church to take seriously the operation of God in current
history. The fact would appear that God's initiative and man's
response to it is today more evident in the life of the world than
in the activities of the Church. The God-man transaction has
by-passed the Church. Undreamed of advances are taking place
in the growth of human personality and human community, as
well as in science and technology. A vast unsettling of past dependent relationships of peoples is being brought about. Economic and social interdependence are fashioning one world,
whether nation states accept the fact or not. Renascent religions,
such as Buddhism, Hinduism, and Islam, are challenging the
religious colonialism of the Christian Church. Whereas the
Church through its long history has functioned in a slowly

evolving universe, much as United States law emerged from English common law which had its antecedents in Roman law, today the challenge of social change compels radical adjustments of thought and behavior unprecedented in history.

The discernment of God at work in the processes of contemporary history calls for humility of a special sort: the willingness to be led into new patterns of service in a world which is only now emerging. An illustration from the civil rights crisis sheds some light on what this means. White Christian Americans have been able to discover their roles and responsibilities only to the extent that they have accepted the fact that initiative lies not with them but with Negro fellow citizens and churchmen. The recognition that God is choosing instruments of His own rather than the Church to fulfill His will comes as painfully today as it did to Israel of old. An unbelievable outpouring of the Spirit is taking place among the peoples of the world in the quest for freedom and the new sense of dignity which is everywhere manifest. So complete is the preoccupation of the Church with its internal affairs that the discernment of the Spirit in the world around us is scarcely perceived as an issue at all, much less as the principal theological task of the generation.

A second and interrelated failure is the Church's inability to penetrate the thought patterns of the contemporary world. From our earlier discussion, it has been seen that solutions to the threat of nuclear war will be pragmatic and scientific (or at least technological) rather than theological and ideological. That pragmatic choices can be at the same time theologically grounded is only beginning to be perceived in the emergence of a so-called "situational ethics." The post-modern world rejects the philosophical assumptions on which Christianity has classically presented the faith. Whether there are "two cultures," with C. P. Snow, or a variety of disciplines, as seems more likely the case, the fact is that the Church is almost everywhere failing to be in conversation with the new world into which we have moved.

It is surprising that this is so, for the Church has within its membership large numbers of lay persons who are very much creatures of this age, disciplined in the thought patterns of the generation, and active in every area of human enterprise. There is, moreover, a growing body of literature on the ministry or the apostolate of the laity, and a consciousness that our present patterns of church life, particularly at the parish level, are failing to challenge the laity to their vocation as the ministers of Christ's Church in and to the world.

A third and crucial failure of the Church in our day is in the area of the training and refreshment of lay persons, who can as Christians function within the various disciplines of modern thought and technology, discerning the operations of God's Spirit in their primary fields of work, and bringing their faith to bear on the peculiar problems of their discipline. Some laymen spoke to this need in an important paper given at the Assembly of the World Council of Churches in New Delhi:

> Christ is not imprisoned in our churches. Christ is incognito already present in the structures and power systems in which we have to live our Christian life. . . .
> We sometimes have the feeling that you have little understanding for this our solidarity with our non-Christian neighbors and colleagues, because your professional concern is so much concentrated on the Church when it is assembled for corporate worship, witness and service. You often press us to become quite consciously the light of the world, to be known as Christians, to form Christian cells in the world of our work and neighborhoods. Often such reminders are quite necessary. But more often our Christian obedience demands us to remain incognito and thus to serve Christ.[9]

Finally, and perhaps basic to each of these other points, is the failure to take seriously the power of the Gospel. Caught in the midst of turbulent changes, many Churchmen doubt the ability of the institutional church to rise to the moral crises of our time, and thereby conclude that there are no solutions to the problems unleashed among us. But God is not thus mocked. He continues to will the unity and peace of His creation. But the terms of the dialogue between Creator and creatures have startlingly changed. The discernment of the ways by which God is seeking to lead the children of men to peace is one of the principal tasks before the Church today.

A faithful attempt to seek peace would undoubtedly cause a revolution in the Church's thought and life. It might open us to a fresh showering of the Spirit and bring the Church nearer to the world for which Christ died.

NOTES

[1] Pope John XXIII, *Pacem in Terris*, Paulist Press, New York, p. 5.

[2] From a special roundup in *Intercom* (Foreign Policy Association), Vol. 5, No. 2, p. 40.

[3] *Ibid.*, p. 9.

[4] Copies of this statement available from Episcopal Church Center, 815 Second Ave., New York, N.Y.

[5] *Cf.* Paul Ramsey, *War and the Christian Conscience*, Duke University Press, 1961.

[6] Roland Bainton, *Christian Attitudes Toward War and Peace*, Abingdon Press, 1960, p. 253.

[7] A notable exception is the Commission of the Churches on International Affairs of the World Council of Churches.

[8] From an address to a convention of the Religious Education Association.

[9] Klaus von Bismarck, E. V. Mathew, and Mollie Batten, "The Laity: the Church in the World," *Ecumenical Review*, Vol. XIV: No. 2, January, 1962, pp. 205-6.

20. Local and National Politics

RICHARD E. BYFIELD

In a recent presidential election, the noted clergyman, Dr. Norman Vincent Peale, acting as a spokesman for a group of Protestant clergy, advised against the election of a particular Roman Catholic candidate. As his statement received national publicity, criticism gathered about his head, to the point that he felt it necessary to repudiate his connection with the organization. He was criticized for a number of reasons, but chief among them was the charge that, in making this statement, he had somehow violated the "principle of separation of church and state." The public at large did not seem to be sympathetic with what he had done, and much furor resulted.

Yet, a year or so later, the Supreme Court of the United States, in the now famous New York Regents' Case, held that it was not the province of one of the several states to write prayers for use in the public schools. This decision, which was made in the name of upholding the principle of separation, was also roundly criticized by press and pulpit; so heavily criticized indeed that there has been a serious attempt in the Senate of the United States to write a substitute amendment which would presumably ameliorate the principle.

In the two incidents cited, public opinion would seem to have reversed itself. The very principle which was used against Dr.

Peale by the public was deprecated by the same public when the Supreme Court referred to it as precedent.

This ambiguous reaction of the American people to the question of separation of church and state serves to illustrate the difficulty that arises whenever one attempts to consider the role of the Church and Churchmen in regard to local and national politics. Whatever position one takes in regard to this relationship, it will be seen as wrong-headed by some. Either the "traditional" American position is not as clear as some would think, or else we must assume that there is a fair-sized body of opinion which really stands against the "traditional" position. The fact that the United States Senate has held hearings looking towards revising the First Amendment would seem at first glance to give some weight to the latter hypothesis; but the fact is that even those who would revise the First Amendment claim to be doing it in the name of the "traditional" position. To my knowledge no one has openly suggested that the tradition itself is wrong and should be changed. Instead, the Supreme Court's critics, at least, have simply held that the Court itself does not understand what the principle really is.

With this confusion existing in the United States, one must also take note of the fact that, while a theology of politics which was applicable to the American Constitution would be of most interest to Americans, there are Christians who have to function under governments which have no tradition of separation of church and state, and even under governments which act in various ways to place disabilities upon the Church. In the interests of brevity, this writer will confine himself to the American scene; contenting himself with "filing by title" the notion that, while the theology really remains the same, the techniques of Christian political action would have to be quite different in, say, Spain or the Soviet Union.

In thinking of Christian political action in the United States, one axiom would seem to be clear: namely that a member of the Christian Church is at least as much a citizen of the United

States as anyone else. Therefore, any suggestion that by becoming a Christian one has necessarily removed oneself from the political scene, would be nonsensical. Yet, far from being a straw man, precisely this argument is often used, particularly against clergymen who express a political viewpoint. Unless one has misunderstood the issues completely, this was the argument used against Dr. Peale; that, as a clergyman, he had forfeited the right which belongs to him as an American citizen to express a political opinion. It is hard to see how this position could be logically sustained.

If we grant that Christians, including clergymen, still have the rights and duties of American citizens, then we should ask what these rights and duties are. In the particular field with which we are concerned, it would seem that Thomas Jefferson's ideal of "pressure groups" within a democracy is most relevant. Jefferson did not visualize a two-party system. Instead, he foresaw a situation in which, whenever an issue was before the public, new groupings of citizens would be formed to work for one side or the other of the issue. When the issue was resolved, the groups would presumably disband, and form new alignments when new issues arose. A necessary concomitant of this doctrine would seem to be that, in such a political system, groups which existed for other purposes would, on occasion, also find themselves taking political positions, when matters which they conceived to be their own interests were involved. Certainly there is nothing either in the Constitution or in the writings of the Founding Fathers which would suggest otherwise.

Since the United States government, under its Constitution, can have no "ecclesiology," it would seem bound to view the churches simply as "groups of people in mutual association." If this is the case, then these groups which we call churches also have neither more nor less right, as citizens' groups, than have frankly secular groups to make their positions known to those in authority. In short, in the eyes of government, a "church" is merely a group of people come together for their own purposes which may function like any other group in the society. No construction of the "doctrine of separation" would indicate that these groups, and these groups alone, could *not* hold political views.

Certainly there are dangers to political activism in the name of the Christian religion, and these must not be overlooked. It would be this writer's thesis, however, that there are equal dangers in non-involvement, and that these must not be overlooked either.

In its simplest frame of reference first, consider the duty of the individual Christian, summed up in our Lord's command "to love one's neighbor as oneself." Anyone who has attempted to take this commandment seriously has soon realized that, in a complex society, one of the most effective ways in which this commandment can be carried out is often the way of legislation. One can resolve personally to make no discriminations as regarding race, creed or color; but if one is to see this view implemented on a scale large enough to make it effective, one will begin to think in terms of fair employment practices acts, fair housing laws, etc. One can easily resolve that he will, personally, allow no one to starve in his presence; but, once again, if people who are really starving are to benefit from this sentiment, it may well be that the sentiment will have to be implemented with welfare legislation, Aid to Needy Children, and legislative acts of this type. To do no murder is a fairly easy item of personal morality; but if one feels that murders done in his name are equally reprehensible, the only way in which this practice can be stopped is to pass legislation which will abolish capital punishment—and, hopefully, such manifestations of mass murder as atomic war. In short, personal individual morality inevitably leads one, and quite rapidly, in the direction of corporate morality, and while it is perhaps true that "morality cannot be legislated," it remains a fact that the moral or immoral *acts* of the society are susceptible, at least to a degree, to legislation and to nothing else. A person must either adopt a completely separatist position for himself, in which he decides to ignore the evils of the society of which he is a part, even while he supports them financially and in other ways, or else he must face the fact that, if he personally is to be moral, in the positive sense, he is going to have to act in some ways to try to make the society more moral as well.

At this point, the Christian ethic and the doctrine of the democratic state again approach each other, for the primary claim of the democratic republic upon its individual citizens is that of individual responsibility. Even in a totalitarian state, the Church has always held that the citizen has the right—and indeed perhaps the duty—to revolt, if nothing else. In the democratic republic, however, the right and duty of dissent are written into the Constitution. Democracy stands or falls upon the willingness of individual citizens to be involved in government. When this demand of the state itself is coupled with the demand of the Christian ethic, it is hard to see how the Christian citizen can be anything other than politically active—and in as effective a way as possible.

Local and national politics is, among other things, a matter of power. Those who can join together for common action will, in the nature of things, almost always be more effective than individual citizens each following their own particular bent. To put it as bluntly as possible, if one is to be of maximum effectiveness in politics, one must somehow put himself in a position to reward supporters and punish opponents, speaking, of course, in terms of the ballot box. Thus, if the individual Christian is to exercise political judgment at all, he will almost always do this most effectively in the company of other Christians committed to the same proposition.

To refer to such a point of view as "immoral," as some will do, is, it would seem to this writer, simply to attempt to label immoral the republican system itself. Our friends of the extreme right, who point out that "this is a republic, not a democracy," are right to this degree: that no candidate has a *right* to public office, and that every official should be allowed to serve only so long as he reflects the will of his constituency. There is no element of vengeance or anger involved in voting a man out of public office if he has failed to do this. It is instead the *duty* of citizens and groups within the republic to put in office those who will reflect the wishes of those who have voted for them. This is not, incidentally, to deny the corresponding right and duty of our elected representatives to attempt to change our opinions by education. The concept of "the bloody pulpit" as applied by Theodore Roosevelt to the presidency, applies also to our other representatives. But, in the final analysis, our legislators are *our* representatives, not vice versa. Politics is concerned with power, and there is no excuse for naïveté among Christians about this. Indeed, if Christians continue naïve, they have no right to expect politicians to take them seriously as an opinion-forming group.

By the same token, every issue that comes before a local or national legislative assembly, has powerful pressure groups on both sides. In the State of California, for instance, there is a continual body of pressure brought to bear upon the State Legislature to establish a state-operated lottery for the purpose of reducing corporate and personal income tax. It may well be that the legislators themselves, at any given time, would be personally opposed to such a proposition in numbers great enough to insure its defeat. However, it is almost certain that, if the years were to go by and no strong voice were to be heard on the other side, such pressure would ultimately be effective. It might almost be put on a basis of compassion; if legislators are going to stand for the right against overwhelming pressures, they deserve to have the support of groups who agree with them, and they deserve to have this support expressed in unmistakable terms. In other words, there are always pressure groups in the field, and if the Church declines to enter this field, it has no right to feel either shock or disappointment when the several legislators gradually or suddenly give in to the pressures of those who *are* willing to take part in the legislative process.

With all this there are, of course, many dangers. There is the danger, most obviously, that certain individuals within the Church will attempt to commit the whole Church to some position which doesn't, in fact, express the will of Churchmen.

Each church organization has had this experience, and most have learned to guard themselves against this sort of thing. Depending upon the polity of the individual Church, however, there are channels by which the will of the majority can make itself known—and if the Church will honestly use these channels it will avoid this danger. This does not, of course, exclude the possibility that individual Churchmen will speak out, and that some of these individuals will be clergy.

A danger which is often cited is that of the identification of a church with a particular political party. The writer belongs to a Council of Churches which, for the past several years, has supported quite regularly the position advanced by legislator-members of one of the two major parties. While this seems unfortunate as a public relations matter, the fact is that each issue is approached as an issue, and it is merely coincidental that the views of the party and the Council of Churches have run parallel so many times. Hopefully the party is on constant notice that the Council of Churches is in no way guaranteeing support of its future legislation; and, should it propose legislation which the Council does not feel is to its best interests, party politicians will soon learn that this is the case. It would obviously be wrong for the Council to refuse to take positions simply *because* the legislation was supported by that particular party, and this would be a kind of "partisanship in reverse." If the Church (and individual Christians) will remember that parties are transitory—even in the American political system—while the Church and Christian ethics are eternal, there will be little trouble in avoiding this particular pitfall.

It has been said so often that it appears to be a truism that "the Church should not support individual candidates," and at first glance this would appear to be a sound warning. However, in many instances, a candidate so accurately reflects certain legislative points of view that it is impossible to separate the man from the issues. If, for instance, a church group were irrevocably committed to the abolition of the death penalty, and if the group considered this kind of legislation to be of overriding importance, it would certainly be naïve to withhold support from legislative candidates who were pledged to abolition, or to support those who were pledged to retention. The dangers surrounding endorsement by a church group of a particular candidate are so obvious that they need not be spelled out. Even with these dangers apparent, however, this writer, at least, would not wish to take the position that such a thing may never be allowed to happen. While it is hardly likely, for instance, that an avowed Communist will be running for public office in any of our several states, if such a thing should happen it would seem clearly the duty of churches and individual Christians to oppose him both in terms of democracy and of the Christian ethic. While the reader may disagree, this would seem to be one of the logical conclusions of all that has gone before.

There are, of course, many other considerations, some highly technical, which will occur to anyone who has given any serious thought to the question of Christian political involvement. All of them, however, might well be summed up in the simple concept of "relevancy." In what has been called a "post-Christian era" the Church has, more and more, been accused of being irrelevant to the real lives of men. We have been accused of having answers to questions that nobody has asked. In the United States of America, at least, men "really live" in the realm of politics, and many of the questions they are really asking are drawn from this area of life. Clearly, then, to ignore this area is impossible; unless we wish to see the Church and Christians as irrelevant to the needs and problems of modern man in a modern society.

21. International Politics

LEE A. BELFORD

We believe that God created the world and all that therein is. We did not create the earth—we are only placed here to do God's will. "The earth is the Lord's and the fullness thereof, the world and those who dwell therein" (Ps. 24:1, RSV). Because we believe there is only one God, the source of all things, we are related to all of God's other children. He has made of one blood all the nations of the earth. "Behold, how good and pleasant it is when brothers dwell in unity!" (Ps. 133:1, RSV).

What happens to anybody anywhere in the world is of concern to the Christian, for every man is his brother, a beloved child of God. There is no way, in principle, by which a concern for a man of one's own country can be any different from a concern for a man of another nation. Nationality, in principle, is irrelevant.

We, as Christians, believe that our Lord Jesus Christ died for all mankind, and in His death reconciled all things to Himself. This means reconciliation with one another. Anything which stands between the reconciliation of man with man is a denial of the true reconciliation that comes through Christ. To use a spacial metaphor, the cross points vertically toward God. Horizontally, it stretches out toward men. We can never be related to God in a vertical fashion without being related to our

194

fellow men horizontally. Unless there is an intersection of the two concerns, there is no cross and no Christianity.

Since the rebirth of the Christian missionary movement less than two hundred years ago, Christians have demonstrated their concern for their fellow men in all parts of the earth. Missionaries were sent to those who had never heard the name of Christ, and were proclaimers of salvation in His name. But the missionaries saw Christ in the eyes of those who would never be converted, saw Christ in the eyes of those in need. Hospitals were founded, schools were started, the hungry were fed, and the naked clothed.

The importance of personal and voluntary service to the needy throughout the world cannot be minimized. We should, in the name of Christ, continue to provide aid and support from our personal resources. Through the activities of Church World Service, millions of dollars worth of food, clothing, medicine, and other material aid have been distributed in over fifty countries. American Leprosy Missions, supported by individuals and local churches, offers the best possible medical treatment and rehabilitation to the world's most neglected sufferers. Other agencies too numerous to mention have served areas that are mentally, spiritually, and physically impoverished.

However, the needs of the world are too great to be met merely by personal contributions, regardless of how sacrificial they may be. For example, illiteracy is not only a personal tragedy, it is an economic strait jacket. The World Literacy and Christian Literature Association has done yeoman's service in teaching reading and writing, but the task is too great for any voluntary agency, for there are over 700 million illiterates in the world today, approximately one-half of the total adult population.

The population explosion may pose an even greater problem than the atomic bomb. More than half the babies born this year will not have enough to eat. Countries like India have launched programs of voluntary population control to maintain a balance between human beings and resources. They ask for help, greater help than the Planned Parenthood Federation, church agencies, or foundations can give. The resources of the wealthier nations must be tapped if any sort of effective program of population control is to be instituted.

Although a nation cannot be divorced from its people, a nation is an entity, and as a nation, stands under the judgment of God. Jesus told a story of the final judgment when all the nations should be gathered before the Messianic throne of judgment where they would be separated as a shepherd separates the sheep from the goats. "Then the King will say to those at his right hand, 'Come, O blessed of my Father, inherit the kingdom prepared for you from the foundation of the world; for I was hungry and you gave me food, I was thirsty and you gave me drink, I was a stranger and you welcomed me, I was naked and you clothed me, I was sick and you visited me, I was in prison and you came to me' " (Matt. 25:34-36, RSV). We are accustomed to think of the evaluative criteria in reference to an individual's conduct, and they are certainly applicable, but the text refers specifically to nations. If we think of the judgment as not merely something in the future but as something that occurs within the realm of history, it is especially relevant to international politics.

As a nation we are inclined to forget God. We are inclined to look at our fair land and say in the words of ancient Israel, "My power and the might of my hand have gotten me this wealth" (Deut. 8:17, RSV). The prophets had significant comments for such an attitude. For example, Amos declared that a privileged position is a responsibility. He declared that because of its very privilege, Israel would be judged more severely than other nations.

When Samaria, the capital of the Northern kingdom of the Israelites, was destroyed by Assyria, the prophets interpreted this as a judgment upon the nation. When Jerusalem, the capital of the Southern kingdom, was destroyed by Babylonia, the destruction was also interpreted as an act of God. Even though Assyria and Babylonia had never known God as Israel did, nevertheless

God used them as His instruments of chastisement. It would be consistent with the prophets if we declared that we are being tried and that if we cannot respond morally to the challenge before us, we shall be destroyed. This is a threat and a challenge to the life of the United States as a nation.

The United States and Russia today are at daggers drawn. We assume that the United States is a more God-fearing nation than Russia. We assume that with our constitutional form of government and free elections, we are more democratic. We assume that we have a higher regard for life, liberty, and the pursuit of happiness. But even if by contrast we are the more virtuous nation, just as Israel thought herself more virtuous, this does not nullify the fact that we may be destroyed unless we truly act as if the world were the Lord's and the fullness thereof.

You do not need to be told that the United States is the richest nation in the world today. Representing only six percent of the people of the world, we possess half the income of the world in terms of the goods we consume. But not only do we have most of the bath-tubs, telephones, radios, television sets, and other luxuries, we also possess the largest accumulation of scientific and technical skills. We even have more than we can consume. Our warehouses are loaded with surplus cotton, and in other warehouses, wheat, corn, and other commodities are slowly spoiling. We complain that the Lord has been too generous in providing us with our daily bread. And we still have factories only partially engaged and men eager for more work.

In other parts of the world the situation is entirely different. There are men, women, and children who starve to death each year. There are those who freeze in the winter because of insufficient clothing and inadequate shelter. There are some countries, especially some in Africa, which abound in natural resources but which lack the technical skills and resources to exploit them, technical abilities and resources which we have in abundance.

How can we speak of surpluses when such great needs exist? How can we turn a deaf ear to the call from Macedonia? We can, only if we shut a large part of the world from our concern, and that we cannot do, as Christians.

Actually, the imperatives of Christian morality and the desire for the welfare of the United States coincide in terms of foreign aid. At present the nations of the world are divided into three power blocks, one dominated by the United States, another dominated by the Soviet Union, and a third that exists on the principle of not being aligned with either of the other two blocks. Yet non-alignment is a nebulous state. It is almost impossible for any nation to be really neutral. The non-aligned nations are basically undeveloped and impoverished. The people of these countries look to the people of the United States and ask if we really care for them, if we are really concerned with their hunger, their inadequate shelter, their lack of skill to develop their own resources.

No one is in favor of a "cold" war but such a war actually exists. The two most powerful nations in the world, each with its own satellites, are in a battle to enlist the support of the uncommitted and undeveloped nations of the world.

On the whole, the United States has been generous in its foreign aid. Even though our country has been accused of exploitation, that is certainly minimal today. Most of the nonaligned countries would prefer being our allies, but they will not be committed to us unless we demonstrate that we are committed to them, not merely in military matters but especially in terms of both the necessities and better things of life.

We can increase our aid to undeveloped countries without it hurting at first. But we must increase it regardless of how much it hurts, and that is where the Soviet Union has the advantage. Russia's income is lower than ours, though it is increasing more rapidly. Fifty years ago Russia was a peasant's land while the United States was already highly industrialized. It is possible for Russia to increase the standard of living of its people each year and still have a huge surplus to give away. People are not so sensitive to the cost of foreign aid when their own lot is improving.

If aid to undeveloped nations is increased by the United States, it is conceivable that Americans will have to economize on some of their needless extravagances. Some of the extravagances are viewed almost as necessities. What will the morale of Americans be like if they have to reconcile themselves to a decrease in some of the luxuries of life? If, as Christians, we respond in the name of love to those in need, the sacrifices will not be great. Unless we are prepared to respond out of Christian motivation, then in pride and selfishness the citizens of the United States may demand such curtailments in foreign spending that the cold war will be lost. The situation in the Soviet Union is far simpler. It is easier for a nation to deny its people things they have never had than to deprive them of things to which they have learned to attach a great deal of importance. Will we be willing to make deep personal sacrifices for the sake of others?

Since the existence of the cold war necessitates foreign aid for our national welfare, the question must arise continually as to whether a particular nation is deserving or not. Can a nation be deserving if some of its statesmen are highly critical of the policies of the United States? Is a nation deserving if it talks the Marxist language and dreams of a socialist state? The answer depends upon many factors. For instance, in most of the Latin American countries there is a semi-feudal society with a vast disparity between the extremely wealthy and politically powerful few and the powerless masses who live in the most abject poverty. Radical changes are demanded in the structures of society, such as land reform, taxation on the ability to pay, and social planning to provide better education, food, shelter, and job opportunities for the masses. Those demanding change will inevitably talk of socialism and probably will use Marxist language. To do so does not mean that the users are aligned with the Soviet Union or Communist China. This is an important factor to remember, for if the United States condemns the movements for social change and becomes aligned with the powers now in control, a situation of instability is merely perpetuated and ultimately will force the advocates of social change into a genuine alliance with the communist block nations.

In under-developed countries around the world, there is a growing national self-consciousness. It is easy for the national leaders to blame the more powerful nations for the plight of their countries. The United States is, and frequently will be, criticized as an exploiting nation motivated by greed and determined to frustrate the growth of national life. Such accusations will always demand self-examination as to their validity, and if valid, the injustices should be remedied. In many instances the charges will be found completely without foundation. But false though the charges may be, they cannot be accepted as a reason for the rejection of aid and support so desperately needed.

The United States is involved in a cold war, not for mere national survival but for the survival of values such as those proclaimed in the Bill of Rights. A dilemma is posed by undeveloped countries that desperately need support and yet have not been able to achieve a functioning constitutional democracy. In Africa in particular, new countries are emerging that have had no experience in democracy. With tribal loyalties primary, and education on a primitive level, authoritarian forms of government may be necessary as an alternative to chaos. If such should be the case, the problem posed would be whether our aid would help prepare the way for democracy or retard its development.

The dilemma is accentuated when the problem of aid to countries that actually profess a communist ideology is posed. Yugoslavia, for example, is committed to communism even though it remains relatively free from the dictates of Moscow. Yugoslavia may be justly criticized for its lack of respect for the dignity of the individual and his political and social rights. However, for the United States to reject all overtures for trade agreements would force Yugoslavia into a situation of greater dependence upon the Soviet Union. The problem of the relationship of the United States to Poland is even greater. Poland enjoys a minor degree of independence from the Soviet Union even though it is within the Soviet block. Trade with Poland, and even aid in terms of surplus food, can strengthen Poland's independence. It can be assumed that with more independence, Poland will be able to develop democratic institutions more effectively.

The United States is in a position where it might be expedient to give aid to countries that profess an ideology and form of government to which a democratic ideology is opposed. Where to draw the line, what methods to use in international diplomacy—these are questions that cannot be settled on the basis of power politics in Congress. Freedom must be given to the executive branch of the government to operate on the basis of a continually changing international situation.

Our comments so far have concerned the United States as if it were acting in isolation. Yet underlying all that has been said is the assumption that nations must co-operate with each other. The Alliance for Progress was formed by the United States and all the Latin American countries except Cuba to carry on a program for economic growth and the social improvement of Latin American countries. The Central Treaty Organization of the Middle East (CENTO) was formed for the purpose of mutual security and the establishment of more effective means of transportation and communication. A more advanced step was taken when the European Economic Community (Common Market) was formed with the purpose of removing tariff barriers and encouraging a free flow of goods and services between a number of European nations.

The United States is sufficiently large and possesses sufficient resources to obviate the necessity of participation with other nations in something like the Common Market at the present time. But Canada is restive because so much of its economic life is dependent upon the United States. Rumblings of discontent come from Mexico with the claim that it is merely a satellite of its big, strong neighbor. Great Britain, excluded from the Common Market, must look to the West. The time may well come when a genuine Atlantic community or some other type of community may be demanded. If such a time should come, it would involve some surrender of national sovereignty. Are the people of the United States prepared for such a possibility?

Most of the development of international organizations has occurred where the nations were in the same political block, but there are issues that involve conflicts between nations of different blocks. There must be an arena within which such issues may be fully considered. There must be a global, international organization devoted to maintaining peace, and this involves a concern with the rights of individuals, economic and social matters, and the affairs of states. Such an organization already exists in embryonic form in the United Nations. There is no question as to whether the United States will participate. The question relates to the extent of our participation, the power we are willing to surrender to such an organization, and the goals that we are willing to accept.

The United Nations is limited in its effectiveness because the leaders of the two major power-blocks, the United States and the Soviet Union, believe that they cannot surrender power without jeopardizing values to which they are committed. Yet the United Nations can even now act as a conscience and articulate the feelings of at least the uncommitted nations. The United Nations can propose means of controlling the weapons race; it can cultivate an atmosphere favorable to peace.

Perhaps the United States and the Soviet Union can work out a test ban, for it is to the advantage of both to do so. Who is to arbitrate, though, when the issue is access to Berlin? Or the occupation by the United States of the naval base at Guantanamo? Or the Soviet imposition of a dictatorship upon Hungary? It is quite obvious that a world organization is demanded which can transcend the arbitrary will of a particular nation. The United Nations does not yet have that power. It cannot until the nations of the world are willing to surrender some of their sovereignty.

Perhaps a discussion of international politics that began with the Christian's commitment to serve his neighbor in need, moved to national responsibility in world affairs, considered the development of international organizations, and finally arrived at the necessity for a strengthened trans-national world organization, can be concluded in no more satisfactory way than by referring to *Pacem in Terris* ("Peace on Earth"), an encyclical issued by Pope John XXIII on April 10, 1963. Pope John pointed out clearly that all men of good will must realize that unlimited national authority no longer exists, that the vast changes in the world have created new problems that cannot be handled in traditional ways. He prayed that the United Nations might be made equal to its task—the safeguarding of world peace and of the universal, inviolable, and inalienable rights of all men. He also prayed for a change in the hearts of men.

> May He (Christ) banish from the hearts of men whatever might endanger peace. . . . May He enkindle the wills of all so that they may overcome the barriers that divide, cherish the bonds of mutual charity, understand others, and pardon those who have done them wrong. By virtue of His action, may all peoples of the earth become as brothers, and may the most longed-for peace blossom forth and reign always among them.[1]

NOTES

[1] Paragraph 171 of the English version of *Pacem in Terris* published by the America Press, N.Y., 1963. Reprinted with permission from *America*.

22. Young People in Our Society

WILLIAM A. YON

"Teen-age" is something new. Although it is obvious that every adult went through a period chronologically identified as "the teens," it is also true that for him this period did not carry with it the kind of consciousness of *being a teen-ager* —as distinguished from being a child or an adult—that it does for the young person of the 1960's.

We are given to understand that Shakespeare's Romeo and Juliet were in their teens, but we do not think of them as teenagers. We think of them as young adults, living in an adult world, making fully adult choices, and suffering an adult fate. Tom Sawyer and Huckleberry Finn were no doubt in their teen years, but we do not think of them as teen-agers either. We think of them as older children, living in a child's world, making a child's decisions, and becoming involved in a child's adventures.

Since the close of World War II, we have seen the emergence of an identifiable sub-culture, emphatically distinct from childhood on the one side and adulthood on the other: the teen-age culture, with its own unique style of life. Not long ago when children divided up to "play house," they appointed a mother, a daddy, some children, and the baby. Now the *dramatis personnae* must include "the teen-ager."

The Church is under obligation to penetrate the young person's awareness of himself as a teen-ager, and to penetrate the young person's world. To do so with any positive effect, it must have some real understanding of the situation in which a young person in our society finds himself, and it must also be ready, as on any legitimate missionary enterprise, to "go native" in everything save faith and morals.

Youth are Superfluous

If it is true that in contemporary American society, the measure of a man is his productivity, we are forced to the conclusion that *the young person is superfluous*. His labor is not wanted or needed. Even when he takes a job during the summer or after school, more problems are created than solved when his effort to "do his share" is viewed in broad terms against the high proportion of unemployed adults in our society. The effects of being unneeded and unwanted in relation to those tasks which society says are most important are very deep indeed. They are effects which may be seen in the frivolous emptiness of much of youth culture.

In the early fifties, the student editor of the Harvard College magazine managed to take an unofficial tour of the communist-controlled eastern sector of Berlin. On the basis of what he saw there, he was forced to the conclusion that the young person in that society participates fully in the central aspirations of the communist system, and as a result enjoys both genuine status and high prestige.

He was then moved to paint this contrasting portrait of the American young person: "He is not without purpose, but his purposes are constantly interchanging. He is not without loyalty, but the object of his loyalty shifts with the ebb and the flow of the crowd's opinions and tastes. *The trouble with the American young person is that he is not really anybody. He is just waiting around to become somebody. He is without status in the American scheme of things.*" [1]

Robert A. Gessert of the Department of Religion at Smith College underscores the same point: "All the noise, all the activity, even the violence in youth culture, is not a way of *doing something* nearly so much as it is a way of *doing nothing*, of waiting until the time is ripe for doing something. The problem is compounded by the fact that our society no longer needs or wants the labors of children and young people . . . Energy is available for the tasks to which one may be called, but instead of calling, society says, 'Wait.' " [2]

Our adult society attempts to offer some meaning to the life of the young person by dramatizing and glamorizing the period of preparation through which he is moving as a student, but the appeal is made on the basis of precisely those values in which the student, as a non-producer, is denied participation: "The high school graduate will make 'x number of dollars' more in his life-time than the high school drop-out." But at this point the cat is out of the bag! *The important thing is how much money he will make when he is an adult.* Little wonder, then, that the young person, who at present is neither adult nor able to make much money, attempts to fill the vacuum of his present existence with such bits of meaning as he can find through his own brand-name clothes, his own souped-up car, his own prestige as an athlete, his own sexual prowess.

New Images of Youth

The problem which adult society—including the adult Church —faces in trying to cope with the young person as he moves through this "no man's land" of youth culture is complicated further by certain distorted images of who the young person is. In the minds of some adults there are still vestiges of the *idealist image* of youth. The young person is seen as possessing boundless (and unrealistic) optimism and hope, fired with zeal to bring in the new day of a perfected society. Unwilling to settle for that which is merely possible, he is seen as being determined to achieve the perfect.

Alongside this idealist image of youth there is also in the minds of adults a contradictory image of youth as *juvenile delinquent.* Dr. Edgar Z. Friedenberg, a sociologist whose major

study has been in the area of adolescent group life, remarked to
a conference of Church youth workers that "it is not possible
to discuss adolescence with a group of American adults without
being forced onto the topic of juvenile delinquency." [3] In further
conversation he reported an experience which bore out the point:

> While I was in Colorado last summer, there were two fairly well
> educated, elderly ladies who had heard that I did some work about
> adolescents. They came over and asked if it was true, as they had
> heard, that there was a tremendous rise in the rate of delinquency
> among second-generation Americans. I said I didn't know whether it
> was true and that I didn't think it was possible . . . to find out. . . .
> They absolutely could not understand that I had worked with ado-
> lescents without being an expert in juvenile delinquency.[4]

Having heard these comments by Dr. Friedenberg, this writer
went to a bookstore to buy a copy of his book, *The Vanishing
Adolescent*. I asked the bookstore manager if he had a book by
that title. His reply: "Oh, that must be a book about juvenile
delinquency and things like that."

The fact is that both images, that of the idealist and that of
the juvenile delinquent, are inaccurate and misleading, as most
stereotypes are. The great majority of young people fall into a
vast middle group of those whose aspirations are neither very
high nor very low, whose behavior is neither very good nor very
bad. Based on interviews with a cross-section of more than 3,000
young Americans, Dr. George Gallup reports that "our typical
youth will settle for low success rather than risk high failure.
He has little spirit of adventure." [5]

Dr. Gallup's report suggests that the classic idealism of youth
has been replaced by an almost grim realism. Since one man's
success is in large part measured by the failures of others, it becomes an inescapable fact that not all may justifiably aspire to
"high success." But more important than the limitations which
a young person must face as regards his prospects for future
success or failure, are the even more severe limitations upon the
possibility of his making a significant contribution while he is
yet a young person. These limitations induce an apathy which
the Church must expect as its first hurdle in its attempt to pene-

trate the world of the young. It is an apathy which has captured the young person as he has come to realize that in terms of the most compelling goals to which our culture has given itself, he is "not really anybody. He is just waiting around to become somebody." So why "sweat" it? Why not be as comfortable as possible until it is time to be somebody?

The Ability to Respond

The chief complaint of American adults is that young people are irresponsible. There are grounds for the complaint. While high school and college youth in South Korea were leading riots that lead to the overthrow of the discredited regime of Syngman Rhee, the *cause celebre* among American youth was to see how many of them could get into a phone booth at the same time. The charge of irresponsibility, however, fails to recognize either the extent of the young person's disenfranchisement as a citizen and Churchman or the meaning of the word *responsibility*.

Responsibility is the *ability to respond* inwardly, to a need outside one's self. When a demand is imposed from the outside it becomes an obligation, a duty, calling for obedience perhaps, but not for inner response. For the young person to be enabled to respond, it must become clear to him that there is something that really needs doing, which *only he* can do. None of the trumped-up youth projects of our churches and communities, which are devised to "make Johnny feel needed," can meet these conditions.

That young people are able to respond under these conditions is evident from the tremendous response to the American Peace Corps. Several factors that lie behind this response are worth noting. In a world marked by deteriorating international relationships, it was obvious that somebody needed to do something for a reason other than what he could personally get out of it. So the Peace Corps volunteers offer their services for subsistence pay. This kind of sacrifice is simply not a possibility for most persons with family and economic obligations, so only those who do not have such obligations can meet the need. And young Americans by the thousand have been *able to respond.*

The Young Church in Action

The central thrust of the Church into the world of the young, then, must be through those *young Churchmen* who are coming to know themselves as Christians, who are coming to realize that God has set them down into a unique slice of the world where there are needs to be met, needs which will not be met if they do not meet them. It should be clear that the emphasis at this point is not on pulling young people into the multitude of operations necessary to maintain the institutional Church, but rather on helping the young person identify his own responsibility as a Christian in the world, his own world of school and family and ball-field and drive-in and, if such be the case, street gang.

The success of most of the Church's efforts at youth work has been measured by the extent to which the Church has been able to withdraw the young person from his life in the world to get him busily involved in activities in the parish house: folding bulletins, cranking the mimeograph machine, making Palm Sunday crosses, or even participating in the Parish Visitation Committee. The institutional Church is in no danger of dying, but there is a world outside the Church which is dying daily, young people dying along with the rest, for lack of meaning in their present existences, dying for lack of hope of a significant future. Young Churchmen who are coming to know themselves as Christians are beginning to discover that when their lives are seen in light of the Gospel, *they are somebody.* They, too, are those whom God loves. This reality is not held in trust until age twenty-one. The meaning and hope of it are as available to the young as to the old. With it goes a mission, as serious and demanding for the young as for the old, a mission to love and serve that world which God loved so much that He gave His Son to die for it. For young Christians this means to love and to serve those persons whose lives happen to touch their own, for they are the young person's world.

It is now a well established strategy of the Church's missionary expansion in foreign places to seek to encourage an indigenous native leadership, and not to keep a new church forever dependant upon "foreign missionaries." In the Church's mission with youth, adults are and will always remain "foreign missionaries." If some adults accept the responsibility of going native with youth, modifying their own tastes and behaviour to some extent in order to communicate the Gospel to youth, it is for the ultimate purpose of raising up some "native Christians"—youth, in this case—who are ready to take up the mission of the Church in their own land, ministering the love of God to one another for the Gospel's sake.

He stands in judgement upon our failure to live as brothers one of another, in the community, the nation, and the world. And we must hear His word of judgement, if we are not to give up our very humanity. We must hear His word of judgement lest we forget and forego our responsibility—our answerability— which lends the dimension of meaning to our lives here and now.

NOTES

[1] Quoted by Ralph McGill in *The Atlanta Constitution*.
[2] Robert A. Gessert, "Youth Culture—What is It?" *International Journal of Religious Education*, copyright Division of Christian Education, National Council of Churches.
[3] 1962 Seabury House Consultation on Youth Work. Transcripts available from Youth Division, National Council of the Protestant Episcopal Church, New York City.
[4] *Loc. cit.*
[5] "Saturday Evening Post," December 23 and 30, 1961. Articles by Dr. George Gallup and Evan Hill.

23. University Education

MICHAEL P. HAMILTON

If the human race does not destroy itself, it is in the intellectual life of our country that we have the opportunity, if not the destiny, to shape the events of the world for centuries ahead. From this perspective the American universities come to focus as institutions of extreme importance.

The need for the Church to be actively participating in the intellectual and social life of a campus is, nevertheless, an issue debated both by Churchmen and those within the universities. This debate is itself a symptom of what is the intellectual crisis of the Western world. We are a nation that has forgotten its religious roots and have presumed that our civilization was born only of natural seeds. While we see around us in the hospitals, political institutions, and the whole enterprise of science, the fruits of the Judeo-Christian religion, and to a lesser degree the Greek culture, these traditions are not understood or appreciated for what they are. The Christian life is reduced to an ethic. The Church, so long associated with education and in some periods its sole guardian, is considered to be a social institution offering an optional loyalty. What a judgment it is that in a nation where there is no other compelling meaning or purpose available to guide our national and individual lives, the religious tradition that has provided the goals and motivation for our civilization, is considered by so many to be irrelevant!

211

The reasons for this apostasy are not such as would warrant us throwing up our hands in despair at the irrationality or sinfulness of mankind. There seem to be three major causes for this state of affairs peculiar to American history, and a fourth that is of European origin. The first is that membership in a denomination for Americans was largely determined by their emigrant status. Instead of religious affiliation being the product of a free flow of ideas that would modify family allegiances, for reasons of conserving cherished European roots, denominations became conservative of their past rather than motivated to relate themselves to a contemporary and evolving society. Secondly, partly because of frontier conditions and the theological instability of independent congregations, great numbers of American Protestants found their source of inspiration in biblical fundamentalism. When this sadly inadequate intellectual approach was accompanied by a strict puritanical ethic, there came to be, and still remains, as anti-human an expression of Christianity as one might choose to imagine. The third important religious influence in our land is that of the Roman Catholics. Here again factors, largely the result of selective emigration, produced an unhappy blend of defensiveness, isolationism, and intellectual rigidity that has characterized much of that church's life up to this decade.

The fourth cause for the alienation of the American intellectual today stems from what he does remember of Western history and of the conflicts which the Church had with new learning. It is a grim judgment upon Churchmen that they persecuted the prophets of science. Since the second World War and the dropping of the atomic bombs, there has been a *rapprochement* between the scientists and the theologians. A convention of "letting bygones be bygones" has permitted limited dialogue between them, a dialogue motivated more by fear of human destructiveness than by love of each other. If a particular conversation takes an unwelcome turn for the scientist, his latent anger is likely to be revealed by his calling attention to the plight of Copernicus, Galileo, Darwin, Freud, and other martyrs.

Irrelevant as this recollection might be, it serves to halt the discussion at that point.

It is true that most denominations have accommodated their theology to past secular learning. Nowadays the shoe is more often on the other foot, and the Ph.D. in a scientific field is more likely to be ill-informed and critical about Christianity than the average cleric is about science. But the conflicts continue and, as always, it is on the frontier of new discoveries that most of the persecution takes place. The educated secularist can find plenty of examples to illustrate his case that Christians have not understood their own doctrine of Creation. The churches have yet to be convinced that this is really God's world, and that all truth about it must be His too. Within the orbit of believers, Biblical critics had a hard row to hoe before they got a fair hearing. Teilhard de Chardin's writings on evolution were suppressed during his lifetime. Biochemists working to produce and control life are in jeopardy of being labelled blasphemers. Birth control information is not available in some States because of a thirteenth century theological system still dominating one religious body. We should recognize that responsible scholars and authors still have cause to feel threatened by ecclesiastical persecution. Rather than feeling free to bring his offering of work to the altar, rather than looking to the Church for a source of support and stimulation, the artist or the scientist, so often bruised in previous encounters, is likely to avoid thinking about the connections between his work and the Christian faith.

The University

When one examines the life of the universities, one finds the elements spoken of in the nation at large mirrored within the intellectual and administrative life of the campus. We have relatively well-qualified scholars teaching, our laboratories are equipped, and our libraries are good. If these facilities are not quantitatively large enough to handle the expected growth in students, increased financing and timely planning can solve most

of the difficulties. But the question of the quality of the education raises more difficult problems. What is the purpose of
higher education? What is to be the priority of goals for the
Administration? When is a student educated? How much Hu-
manities should be included in the curriculum of a science or
professional degree? How much Science should be included in
a Bachelor of Arts degree? What is the relationship between
disciplines, and how can it be made apparent to the student?
Should the growth of a department be determined by the financial grants that are received, or by an Administrative decision
based on educational policy? Should a university have, as its top
priority, service to community and national needs, or the teaching of traditional bodies of knowledge and the practice of basic
research? What weight is to be given in the hiring and promotion of faculty to their publications, and what weight to
their teaching skill? How much emphasis and administrative
time is to be given to the athletic activities of students? What
kind of students will be granted admission, and what facilities
for extra-curricular activity will be available for them? These are
all questions that raise deep philosophic and religious issues.
Decisions made in these matters will determine the quality of
life in the academic community and in the nation. Students
have very little influence in the framing of these decisions.

For the student, the university has become primarily a step-
ping stone to his chosen field of work. His interior life is concerned with the quest for self-discovery. Moving out of his family
life into a new found freedom and responsibility, he has to test
his judgment about making friends, choosing courses, forming
his opinions about the knowledge he is acquiring, and re-examin-
ing the values which have shaped his life in days before. At first,
frightened to be in a strange community, he is likely to maintain loyalties which have given him previous support. He will
write his parents frequently, leave campus for home as soon as
classes end, and continue to attend church on Sundays if that
has been his practice. Within a month or so, his friendships and

associations will provide him new security which permits the ruthless testing of past convictions. He will rebel against former undesired restraints, and drop those beliefs, religious and social, which no longer seem useful in his present existence. What beliefs will he adopt to replace those inherited? Here in the mind of the student rages the same battles that we found to exist on the national and university policy levels. The most important influence upon the student while he seeks his new values are the faculty. They are the appointed authorities; they are the spokesmen for what Truth is available. Their influence is felt far beyond the limits of the discipline they teach.

The faculty are the core of a university. They provide in their function and person the continuity of the academic community from one generation of students to another. While the changing demands of society upon the university are visited upon the administration and trustees, the faculty, by the accumulation of knowledge within their minds, are the stabilizing element. They are the memories of society, storehouses of unevaluated and unrelated material occasionally, but they and the books they write represent the raw material of civilization.

It is the property of raw materials that they can be fashioned into a variety of artifacts according to the purposes of the workman. By the same token, scientific and historical facts do not carry their own interpretation, but rather ask for a meaning to explain their interrelation and an ethic to guide their utilization. Why is a particular subject matter worthy of examination? Is the teacher aware that he has assumptions underlying the methodology of his discipline? What are the presuppositions affecting his selection of material within his subject matter? What are his views on the nature of man? What is the extent of his responsibility to his students? In the course of a week's lectures, a student can be exposed to factual material taught through faith in Scientific Humanism, Logical Positivism, Economic, Biochemical, or Economic Determinism, Christianity of a variety of levels of sophistication, Atheistic and Theistic Exist-

entialism, and Avowed Neutrality or Objectivity! No wonder
the students are confused, particularly if the process of philosophic exposure is unconsciously given and received.

The personal life of the faculty man is no peaceful haven in
which he may easily find time and resources to make up his own
mind in relation to these matters of faith. Until recently he was
grossly underpaid and unrespected by the society he serves.
Within his department he is involved in the highly competitive
struggle for promotion. He will be torn between his responsibilities to his family, the need to publish, his concern for his
students, and the demands that are made upon him to serve on
administrative committees. A great deal of his life will be determined for him by the essential demands his profession makes
upon him, and the necessary time it takes any man to eat, sleep,
and live in society. But there are variable factors in his life
which will be crucial in permitting or obstructing the fulfillment
of his natural talents. The number of students in his class will
affect how he can teach, specifically whether he has to lecture
or can engage in dialogue. For how many courses will he have
to prepare notes? Will he have time to read outside the realm
of his own specialty? Who are his associates? Will he form
friendships with men outside his discipline, and have the energy
and courage to expose his learning to theirs? How much freedom
will the university permit him to engage in controversial issues
of the day?

The Administration determines whether the talent in the
faculty and the students can flower or not. According to the administrators' understanding of the purpose of the university, how
much they respect truth and justice in matters of discipline, how
efficiently they oversee clerical functions, their exercise of these
powers will make or break the spirit of their community. They
are usually the busiest and loneliest men on campus. Theirs is
the responsibility to make decisions which will make one party
disgruntled and the other feeling he has received only what he
deserves. They are the middle men between society and scholars,
and they are deeply involved in ideological disputes and personal

struggles for power. No longer having the time to keep up with scholarship in whatever discipline they began their careers, they are pressed by the demands for the expansion of facilities and the financial, legal, and architectural problems that such growth entails. They juggle political, social, and academic obligations. They are likely to view their work as constant attempts to forestall crises. The temptation for the President is to give up the struggle to administer a broadly based policy, and to devote his energies to promoting an image of the university pleasing to society. In the interests of providing a viable budget, academic considerations can easily be sacrificed for short term public relations.

The Church

This brief account of the importance and complexity of university life should illustrate the need for the Church to provide a ministry of appropriate depth and commitment. It is a pathetic commentary upon present lack of vision when the work of a Chaplain is judged in terms of student attendance at services, Confirmation classes, and Sunday night suppers. If the description of university life is weighted with the problems rather than the glories of that institution, it is well to recall that it was because of sin rather than righteousness that our Lord entered the arena of human affairs. God came to us as a man; He did not ignore our plight or shout advice to us over the ramparts of Heaven. It was for love, and not for condemnation, that Christ was born into the world He had created. It is in the recognition of these acts that the Church can discover its posture towards the university and the world. The Church must love the university, cherish its learning, give thanks for its existence, and provoke it to self-examination. Representatives of the Church, lay and clerical, should be willing to immerse themselves in the life of the university, to learn from the university, and to treat each of its members as individuals whom Christ deemed worthy of a costly redemption.

Most of the work of God the Holy Spirit on campus is being

done through laymen, whether they are students, faculty, administrators, or janitors. A Chaplain is but one member of a team who ministers to that small percentage of souls that cross his path. For many years our Chaplains spent their time handing out theological band-aids to students injured at the hands of faculty. Gradually we have become aware that faculty are also humans, with personal and intellectual problems that call for special attention. Changes in their orientation to their subject matter and to religion have enormous effect upon those whom they teach.

There are other aspects in a total Church ministry. The presence of foreign students in our land presents very important opportunities for responsible service. We have yet to find effective means of reaching out to those in commuter colleges. Many American non-Christians are in need of assistance of one kind or another, and the churches are now awake to the fact that a campus is also a missionary field. Unhappily some churches have never progressed beyond an understanding of their ministry as one of simple evangelization. Their representatives rush around as spiritual head-hunters roaming the campus for membership scalps. This does not endear them to the administration or faculty, whose suspicions that the churches are concerned for themselves alone and not for the enterprise of education, are thereby confirmed.

What are the marks of a responsible Christian ministry within a university? The student, concerned for self-knowledge and discovery of what it means to be a man or a woman, wants to be assured that this is a worthwhile venture, and needs to be challenged to respond to what is best in him and in the Christian tradition. He will have doubts about his religious beliefs, and should be provided with material about the Christian faith on the level of his growing secular scholarship to enable him to make his decisions in the freedom of knowledge. Doubts provide opportunities for religious growth. He needs to learn that, in spite of his empirical attitude of mind, "proof" of the truth of Christian faith is not available, necessary, or desirable. All we have is enough revelation from God for our salvation, and enough evidence of that revelation to permit a reasonable and intellectually honest trust. Questions about other religions, ethics, the existence of evil, and the need for a purpose for his life will crowd his mind, and he will be the better for having opportunities to discuss them openly. Theologically informed faculty can engage in these conversations and work as effectively as a Chaplain.

The Chaplain serves as a catalyst for others to re-appropriate their lost cultural and religious heritage. His definitive function is to be found in his priesthood; it is as the one who celebrates the Eucharist and offers the Sacraments of the Church that he can recognize his peculiar vocation. His responsibility is also to preach the Gospel, and that means that he has to understand the ways of man as well as of God, so that he can have a ministry of genuine reconciliation. He must be willing and competent to deal with all kinds of churchmanship, able in his personal life as well as his formal acts to convey the love and forgiveness of God. He cannot be expected to be competent in any discipline but that given him in his theological training. He should be able to recognize those points where Christian truth impinges upon secular learning, and have sufficient grasp of technical terminology to clarify the questions for those who must answer them for themselves. This means, for example, that he should be concerned for the question of the nature and limitation of human freedom as it occurs in psychology, economics, and history, as well as in moral theology. He is to ask leading questions, to provoke discussion about neglected and perhaps profound issues, and to avoid the premature giving of answers.

Parish clergy, by and large, only meet people who want to meet them. On campus a Chaplain will be drawn into encounters with those who feel no obligation to respect his collar, and who have no reservations about the honest expression of their feelings towards Christianity. As a Chaplain one is able to know the measure of the world's hostility towards the Church in quite explicit terms.

Most students and faculty see no relevance between what they are doing on campus, and the activities of the parishes from which they have come or are attending. Students arriving on campus expect religious gatherings to be dull, hypocritical, concerned with pious prattle, and so they generally avoid contact. This is a judgment both upon the culture and the Church. As long as our national culture is sub-Christian, post-Christian, or whatever one may decide to call it, even the most gifted cleric, on or off campus, cannot expect to make but a small dent in patterns of thought and behavior. We are reaping the harvest of centuries of obtuseness and disunity within the universal Church. But as long as the Church sees this impasse in terms of the sin of individual men, as opposed to a general intellectual disillusionment, it will continue to flounder in irrelevant remedies. Christ is not the answer to all questions, only the profound ones. It took God nearly two thousand years to prepare the Jews to meet their Messiah—and even then most of them chose to kill Him. It will take us time to prepare our culture again to receive its Lord, to aid men to ask the Judeo-Christian questions. An Indian student expressed the predicament of twentieth century man quite well when he remarked: "The world does not know where it is going; it is like a letter with no address."

In spite of feelings of helplessness, lack of meaning, and cynicism in the face of political realities, the student today is very much concerned about the affairs of the world. If the Christian students are told by their Chaplain or ecclesiastical superiors not to organize pressure groups to remedy social injustices, they will leave the Church and not the world. This is the generation of Freedom Rides and the Peace Corps. Students may not be idealistic, but neither are they inactive, and Chaplains, to be truly incarnational, have to be with, if not to lead, those to whom they attempt to minister. Students are distrustful of organized religion because of the apparent inflexibility of ecclesiastical institutions. We need a new freedom and spirit of daring. God is working His purposes out in the world; we Christians must have sufficient sensitivity to recognize Him, and enough energy to join His agents. When Church leaders, lay and clergy, have enough courage to incur the anger of the privileged for the sake of justice to the downtrodden, our worship and establishments might be more acceptable to God and men.

The first task of the Church in ministering to faculty, or to graduate students who are the next generation of faculty, is to regain their trust and respect. Mention should be made here of the imaginative and pioneering endeavors of the Church Society for College Work. This Society, privately supported, has for the past decade given leadership by experimenting with ways of ministering to faculty in universities, medical, and law schools. They have provided funds for Chaplains in large universities to work specifically with faculty and graduate students, and have held very successful Summer Schools in Theology for university personnel. At these Schools, faculty, under the guidance of competent theologians, meet to study, worship, and live together. They learn what is the relevance of the Christian tradition to the discipline they teach. Some from these Schools have been given grants to do further study, not that they might become ordained clergy, but that they may be better equipped as lay Christians working and witnessing in the heart of the universities.

Because the churches have alienated so many of the learned, we bear their hostility upon our shoulders. Until we Christians are willing to be utterly honest intellectually, honest about moral failings, honest about the errors of the past, we cannot expect them to listen to us. A Chaplain must earn his way into the confidence of faculty and be prepared to converse on subjects that concern them, rather than what he believes they should be interested in! A professor may be a scholar in his field, and yet his understanding of Christianity may be no better than that of a fourteen-year-old. A Chaplain must listen for hours to laments both just and unjust, and while he can correct factual errors, he must be willing to absorb the hard feelings that are released. He must be free from mental fear, know that God has no need of being defended and that the Church has much to learn from

its critics. He must have faith that a radically free relationship
between men provides the greatest opportunity for the Holy
Spirit to work.

Once trust has been established and basic misunderstandings
about the faith removed, progress is possible. Faculty then become open to Christian literature, experience new depths in
worship, make contacts with other Christian faculty and with
members of the Department of Religion, if the university is
fortunate enough to have one. The questions about the nature
of man, the presuppositions of their discipline, the values they
have been communicating as they teach, can be identified and
compared with Christian insights. If a professor has not been
mentioning the religious issues that surround and penetrate his
subject, he may see that he has been implying that they do not
exist, or are not important. If he has claimed an allegiance to
Objectivity as reason to avoid these issues, he can be reminded
that the pedestal of Objectivity can rest only on the ground of
Truth. To discover this domain he must choose between many
so-called truths the world offers him, and realize that this choice
takes place in the milieu of the issues he has wished to ignore.
If he pleads Neutrality or Agnosticism on some questions, he
may be granted breathing space! However, it should be pointed
out that his resultant inactivity will permit the continuance of
the very ills he is likely to be reacting against.

A professor cannot preach the Gospel in the classroom, but
he can be a modern John the Baptist, preparing the way of the
Lord, by encouraging students and associates to see the depths
of the subject they are studying. This in no way violates the
canons of academic responsibility. It is so much easier to talk
about what men did, than discuss why they did it; it is easier to
describe how things behave, than to take time to ask what
should be done with the knowledge; but when questions of
meaning and responsibility are excluded, education is never total.
Once these dialogues are begun, faculty may wish to continue
them amongst themselves. Political scientists, classicists, engineers, psychiatrists, and physicists, can argue and deliver papers

to each other on questions in common. Small miracles occur from such interchange; men esteem their discipline afresh for the particular contribution it makes to the solution of a general problem, and they become glad again to teach. They begin to see the relationship of what they are doing to other disciplines and to the historical process, and exciting intimations of a genuine unity of truth are felt. Thus a university comes that much closer to self-consciousness, to a sense of purpose, and to an understanding of the ways it can serve our confused society.

The Church cannot and should not tell the administrators what precise paths a university should follow. No one knows what the outcome of the present international struggles will be, or what effect new scientific discoveries will have on human society. Christians can provide insights and values which are essential so that a university can be caught up in its own vocation, in whatever world remains to us. The Judeo-Christian tradition is still as fresh, dynamic, profound, and enhancing of man's freedom as ever it was. Man has significant choice in the determination of his fate in this life; Truth is not contradictory, regardless of how many different mouths pronounce it; Reason and Nature are trustworthy; Reality is more than can be measured and weighed; and men are to be forgiven as well as fed. These verities are life-blood to education and research.

This is the age of the turbulent city, a time when the world is in crisis not peace, a time when men are afraid. Christians know only that the future is still God's time. Our joyous service is to stand within the world—and its universities—and hold the hands of nonbelievers until their eyes are opened, and they see the God that stands by all of us.

24. Justice

JAMES G. JONES

> . . . Never send to know for whom the bell tolls; it tolls
> for thee.

The bell tolls all right—but in a dead, clangy sort of
way. The thud of nearly two million doors slamming on a year's
crop of criminals in the U.S.A.

The bell tolls again—a cash register dinging off $22 billion
(whatever that means), F.B.I. Chief Hoover's estimate of annual crime costs.

The bell tolls like the soft ding on the typewriter carriage.
Inmate "X" is typed and retyped on a prison arrival sheet as he
continues to come back seventy-two per cent of the time, only
again to join the numbered ranks of the typical U.S. prison: too
large to produce anything but anonymous, nameless, de-baptized
members, and too cheap to pay for anything but underpaid
guards who think psychiatrists, sociologists, criminologists, pe-
nologists and trained chaplains should be found only in universities.

These prisons are so steeped in security measures that little
time is left for rehabilitation, even if there were professional
teams at work. Prisons are so numbed in idleness that less than
one-third of an average population is involved in prison industry,
so atrophied that the only rejoicers are the strange marriage
partners: the manufacturers' associations who want nothing pro-

duced in a prison and the unions who want no non-union (and therefore inmate) workers in the prison.

The bell tolls, but not for whom we would think. It tolls for a society with a cancer eating its innards and gobbling Tums for relief.

Why? We have no basic philosophy of crime and punishment. We don't understand cause or cure. We stand on various pragmatic platforms—punitive, deterrent, or rehabilitative—without having searched any deeper.

We cry for the simple answer. "Punish him! Deter him, and the rest like him! Rehabilitate him!" Always we assume it's a simple problem, a problem of right and wrong, black and white; a simple problem which should respond to a simple cure. But it isn't and it doesn't. Crime increases eight to seventeen per cent faster than the population. Deterrence seems to produce nothing but assured rehabilitationists who aren't quite sure *why*, but are sure *what*, rehabilitation is the answer.

Let us try to look deeper. Let's look way, way back to dust and toil, to Adam and Eve.

We can at least admit that our first parents were thieves. They committed petty larceny by stealing apples. The second crime was major, when Cain killed his brother, Abel. This type of homicide is still responsible for eighty per cent of murder today. Moving on to such biblical figures as Abraham and Isaac, we begin to see the standard causes of crime, which still hold true in our times.

Isaac marries Rebecca and in their older years they conceive. Twin boys, Jacob and Esau, are born, and they engage in sibling rivalry from the moment of their birth. Twice the clever Jacob cheats his brother out of his birthright—once over a bowl of pottage and once by disguising himself as Esau to his father. Hate bursts forth. They part and go into far different lands. Jacob meets Rachael by the well and works seven years for her hand, only to be cheated by papa Laban, who slips "tender eyed," ugly duckling daughter Leah under the veil and so marries her off to Jacob.

Not to be undone, Jacob works another seven years to win Rachael, using his time profitably, building up his own herd of cows and depleting Laban's. Finally he steals Laban's belongings and returns to his own land with two wives and their two hand-maiden concubines.

Children are born, and we see the natural next step of criminality in the family life of Jacob—too many wives for the children (*i.e.*, polygamy, practiced simultaneously then, serially now). Children will naturally disintegrate when they cannot find identity in a strong mother-father relationship. Son Joseph portrays this beautifully; he needs ego support, and so carries tales about his father's wives. Jacob apparently sees his needs, and instead of a leather jacket and cowboy boots, gives him a coat of many colors to give him status.

But this doesn't work. Further disintegration takes place. Day-dreams of delusion and hallucination take over: dreams of the sheaves bowing to his sheaf and the stars (brothers) and the sun and moon (parents) doing obeisance to him. Finally the family splits apart in hate. The brothers plot to kill Joseph. Reuben saves his life, however, and Joseph is sold into slavery to the Midianites, the Ishmaelites and then to the Egyptians in the household of Potiphar. The process of banishing a troubled child has taken place; slavery instead of a reformatory.

Again we see one of the common syndromes in criminality, that of possible latent homosexuality. Potiphar's wife tries day after day to get Joseph to lie with her, only to be spurned. In the name of religion, yes, but one wonders how this terribly pious person could do the things he did to his father and brothers later and really be so pious. I think perhaps that his resistance was not as trying for him as we might think.

Joseph finally burns out his hostility, which is the basis of such a syndrome, and, after an agonizing time hurting his family, he brings his brethren down to Egypt. There they face the typical problem that an immigrant culture faces—be it Negro, Italian, Irish, German, Polish or what-have-you. Always there is the dominant group threatened by the minority group, particularly in the area of economics.

The gentleman's agreement of today—"call Negroes 'boy,' and pay them like a boy with a broom"—is the same as "make bricks, but we will give you no straw." Each immigrant group cries out in the name of religion against this persecution, but the Church of the day is always of the dominant group. They have conferences—first a grass roots conference in New York, then a resource conference in Connecticut, and then a national conference in Chicago. But the pressure on the sub-group doesn't let up, so they turn to politics to bash their way out of the dilemma.

Moses was their leader, and like all minority group, political leaders, he walked a thin line between right and wrong, legal and illegal. He was a revolutionary figure. He told his people to spy out where the Egyptians kept their silver, gold, and jewels. When he blew the whistle they would grab this loot and run. But before he had arranged everything, he killed a guard in an act of premeditated homicide. Moses gathered his forces and ran, and the posse couldn't catch them because it was caught in the mud of the Red Sea. Then an interesting thing took place.

Today we speak of the cultural lag process, where it takes about two generations for the sub-culture to catch up to the peer culture. The old sub-culture then does to the next sub-culture exactly what was done to it—all in the name of justice, of course. Moses was in the desert just forty years, two generations, before he had a long talk on top of the mountain and came down with the punitive laws of an eye for an eye and a tooth for a tooth, limb for limb and life for life. He who forty years earlier was the law breaker, now writes and enforces the law, never thinking that if this law had been applied to him, he would have received "10 to 20 years" for criminal grand larceny, or been hung as a murderer.

Some thousand years later, Jesus Christ said that, unlike men of old, he wanted no part of punitive justice. Instead, he favored turning a cheek when hit, to be hit again if necessary, to walk a second mile when asked only to walk one, and to give even your cloak with your coat.

Jesus has been called the eminent teacher, physician, psychologist. I suggest he was the eminent sociologist as well. He knew crime to be a social disease caused by a fallen society. To strike only at the symptom or the victim is never to strike at the cause.

"Unto him that smiteth thee on the one cheek offer also the other." All this means is that to attack crime properly, one must look beyond the offender—one must box the whole circle of the compass as one turns ones head looking for the causes which made the culprit strike in the first place.

Again, let's take a good look at what we have, and the pieces will begin to fall into shape.

The Jacob-Esau syndrome

The problem is sibling rivalry in relation to property, or, better put, in relation to what is mine, or better still, in relation to what makes me. What are my rights in my natural family? in society? Or, in Christian terminology, what is the relationship of me, as an individual endowed with a unique and eternal soul, to all souls united in the Israel of God—the Body of Christ?

The Joseph and mother syndrome

Who is my mother? Apparently we must have a strong and lasting, single mother figure to build an ego strong enough to survive and resist disintegration and criminality. Be it four mothers at once—Leah, Silpoh, Rachael, Bilhoh—or mothers serially by divorce and remarriage, the end is the same, disintegration.

The syndrome seems to follow a regular pattern, usually beginning with internal disharmony. ("I didn't make it with my stepmother.") Then come the acts of grandeur, and the seeking of a mother substitute. At this stage the clothes horse will find the same satisfaction in an Italian cut suit as Joseph found in his coat of many colors. A typical car thief will describe his experience thus: "I saw her sitting under the street light . . . powder blue and shiny . . . what a beauty . . . I got inside her . . . tried the lights, horn, radio . . . jumped the wires, and boy, did she respond . . . purred like a kitten . . . outdragged anything I challenged." The final step is banishment.

Today we don't banish our sons to Midianite slavery; we foster-home them, military school them, youth commission them and incarcerate them; but it's all the same, and so are the results. We encourage a Joseph-type personality—latent homosexual, cruel, semi-psychopathic, doubtful improvable offender.

The Joseph-Potiphar syndrome

Using things for their wrong end is typical of a society producing criminals, and is most easily seen sexually, though it is by no means limited to sex. Mutual love and companionship and the procreation of the species is turned to "kicks," and all kinds of motives for sexual participation and non-participation are given except the right ones.

The first generation immigrant syndrome

Hebrews with Egyptians, Irish with Bostonians, or Negroes with Chicagoans—it's the same old story. No group ever immigrates (D.A.R. notwithstanding) for any other reason than trouble. The Hebrews were starving and went to Egypt. The Irish were out of potatoes and went to Boston. The Sicilian had no work, and the Polish no land. Each new group met the peer group and were promptly "put in their place" because of the economic threat posed. The arguments take different forms— "their religion is bad and they are dirty," "they'll intermarry," "they'll take over," "property values will go down"—but they all boil down to the different ways of selfishly holding on to property at the expense of people.

So we put the newcomers down, herd them into ghettos, call them "boys" or "little Irish girls," so we can pay them like adolescent baby sitters, and the natural results take place—a sub-culture is built that procreates delinquents. It's a simple matter of not belonging. The child doesn't relate with his old country parents. He revolts against the old culture, and tries, but fails to get accepted by the new. The child is caught betwixt and between. He becomes frustrated, acts it out, gets picked up, and we write it off by classifying him as a gang-type (where he finds some acceptance), socially maladjusted, suppressed ego, cross-culturally conflicted delinquent. "Send him away!" (Cf. the song to Officer Krumke in "West Side Story.")

These are the syndromes one sees when he turns his cheek, these and many more. All must be treated, but how? The only way is by walking that second mile, for therapy is essentially a one-to-one relationship between two human being in an act of sharing. Delinquents are too pent-up to lie down on a couch or even sit a counselor's desk and spill out the hostility eating them up. The delinquent must walk, kick, spit, pound his fist. He must be mobilized to vomit out his innards in the treatment process.

The street worker of the YMCA understands this. The walking case worker of St. Leonard's House knows this. The priest— living, eating, sleeping and roaming his community—knows this too (although often his bishop doesn't, as he closes one after another of the inner city parishes). Above all, the prison *doesn't* know this. The prison immobilizes the will, intellect and even the body, and then stares in wonderment at a seventy-two per cent return rate.

Man cannot live by bread alone, nor can he live by graceful treatment done. A prisoner needs clothes (his cloak too), a job, a bed, food, yet we turn them out like cattle to forage in a hostile and dead pasture. Plain old physical help is necessary for the whole picture.

This then, is the Christian platform of criminology. It's not punitive, it's not deterrent or even rehabilitative—it's uniquely Christian.

We must *find the cause*—social and individual. *Treat it*, one-to-one, and attack the underlying social causes. *Bolster it* and help it physically.

Unless we try, the bell will toll death tolls of a society that couldn't handle its criminal problem. If we try, the bell can ring joyously as resurrection takes place in the society. Yet the individual resurrection of a criminal in our society seems so hopeless. The fallen society produces so many more than we can help. As an individual career is a neurosis, cyclical in pattern (like a snake eating its tail), so is the social system suffering from social neurosis in a cyclical pattern. Thus an answer to a sixty-five to seventy per cent Negro prison population is not really civil rights, because it's only a matter of cyclical time before the assimilated Negro culture becomes dominant and has some other minority group to treat as children.

The answer is to cut into the cycle at an individual point, rather like chopping that "endless" snake in two. This is existential incarnation. Only an intrusion into history, a traumatic parting of cyclical history, can treat social neurosis.

This happened in the incarnation of Jesus Christ a long time ago, but continued incarnational intrusion into our sick society doesn't seem to happen because of a lack of understanding of the nature of the historical extension of the incarnation: the Body of Christ—His One Holy Catholic and Apostolic Church. If the Church daily intrudes into history, into economy, into culture or any attribute of the social stream, then the Incarnation of Jesus Christ is continuing its intrusion into history.

Probably one of the reasons the prison system remains so ineffective is that atonement is another aspect of the Incarnation which must become existential in history. Guilt seems to be the basic reason our society prefers to waste people rather than change them. As long as we have a recognizable and located group of guilty ones, we have a wonderful place to project our guilt. The criminal of today stands as the scapegoat of Israel; as the crucifixion of Jesus Christ. Christ's atoning crucifixion was all sufficient propitiation, but a criminal is most insufficient to carry even his own guilt, much less ours.

Why then do we use the criminal instead of Christ? Because he is here today and Christ was around 2,000 years ago. Still, we

can make atonement existential in our daily lives. The Church
has amply provided for daily bloodless sacrificial atonement in
the Holy Eucharist. Here the benefits of the one atonement are
redistributed in the forgiving sacrament of His Body and Blood.
When our social system learns that this method of guilt projection
is capable of handling our guilt, it will stop using its daily method
of crime news reading. Only then will we be able to say, "We
don't need the prisoner for our health; we have found perfect
health in God." Only then will we have the strength to stop
the tolling bell of crime and ring a resurrection bell of treatment.
Until then, we must be satisfied to foreshadow this by individual
treatment of a few criminals, waiting for society to have the
strength to attack the problem on a total scale.

(Gratitude is expressed to Lloyd H. Weston for editorial assistance on this essay
—*the Editor*)

25. Time

MICHAEL ALLEN

As I write, I have ringing in my ears and breaking my heart the horrifying news that four little girls have been bombed to death in their Birmingham, Alabama, Sunday School room. One boy has been shot in the back by a policeman more lost than that child ever was or is now. Another boy shot to death by two white teenagers whose elders, by their hatred and contempt for law, order, and humanity, told them to do this frightening thing.

I know we are all hurt by this—all of us terribly hurt in our humanity, because we did this. It was not the governor of Alabama, though indeed his guilt is heavy. Nor was it a gang of assassins, whomever we some day discover them to be; nor was it that policeman, victim of a system he helped to build. And most of all it was not those two teen-agers, because they were hardly more than children, though they will pay heavily for crimes more truly committed by others.

We are guilty—because we do not know what time it is. We do not know that it is *now*: the forever *now* in which we live and from which no man ever escapes.

There is no past in which we can hide ourselves. No great days when things were better and man less guilty. There is no future, but a present, both terrifying and beautiful, looming over

233

us. There is but this single moment, demanding of us that we
act, that we decide between life and death, hope and despair.

I think of other children going to the schools in my neighborhood: terrible schools where classes are too big, where teacher
and pupil are at each other's throats.

Last Spring one of the boys of my parish ran down a school
corridor. He bumped into a teacher twice his size. The teacher
beat him brutally. When I complained to the principal, he said
he didn't know what I was upset about.

The boys in my senior high school class joke about their
school. They say that periodically the teachers ask for volunteers
to go down into the basement to hold up the school so it will
last another hour.

Can these children wait for us to fix up or replace their schools?
Can they wait while we, with patience and due care, contemplate
the situation, wondering if "they" are going too fast—wondering
if we will have to pay too high a cost. In the meantime the
precious moments slip by for children to learn to read, to learn
to express themselves, to think about life and begin to cope
with its arithmetical complexities. We do not live in the future.
The children do not live in the future. We live *now*, where life
is always centered. What we do with *now*, will determine the
future which is another *now* coming to confront us.

So every moment of every day is filled with the urgency of
time converging upon us. It is not uniquely so now. It has always been so, because every moment was like this. Every moment through history asked of man that he fulfill that moment,
give it meaning, use it.

Late in June this past summer, I received a call from a fellow
priest. It was a very simple call. He told me he was going to
Baltimore on the Fourth of July where he would help integrate
an amusement park. He had pledged himself to accept arrest and
to pay the consequences. Would I join him?

I told him I would think about it and call him back. But I
knew already what my decision was. There was only one choice.
If I did not go, I could never live with myself again.

My *now* had come. The Lord had pointed his finger at me, and if I did not come, then I was never preaching His gospel before.

So I went and faced my present, which grew out of my past. It grew as inevitably as a mustard seed grows into a tree, as surely as that mustard seed was a tree all along. So strange is time, which in the moment reveals what always was.

So now what I do today, what I write today, has the future in it blooming, not yet ready to break forth, but there. I do not know what that future is. God knows. But perhaps I can guess. Perhaps I had better guess.

The moment which I let go by, the action I fail to do because it is too soon, is an action I have failed to do for all eternity because my inaction says there is no seed for the future—or not for that particular seed anyway.

We shall change our schools. They will be better. There will be a *now* in which men can speak proudly of what they have done. There will be a moment when little girls do not get bombed in Birmingham. But that *now* will never come for those who sit in silence and pretend the moment is not addressed to them. It will never come for those who now fight to preserve evil. It will never come because they will no more accept the future *now* than they accept the present *now*. That is the judgment; and it always comes *now*.

The judgment always comes in the things I have done, in the things I have left undone. Which is why a Christian begs God's forgiveness every day for his actions and inactions, praying that they will not shape the future; that the seed was truly something else; that the seed is planted in God's forgiveness.

We know this about time because we know the past so well. We know Jesus Christ crucified at one moment in history. We do not know Him as the eternal Christ before we know Him as the Christ in time and history. He was a man walking the roads of Palestine, a little country, far away in time and space, in a dim moment of the past. But on a Friday in a year we think we know, He died on a cross, and rose again.

His disciples saw their moment with a brilliance which never left them, nor their followers. So we have the New Testament, which lives for us because it says every moment that every man everywhere matters—matters desperately, because there is never any other moment more important than this moment in which we live.

In my parish we join for the Holy Meal of our Christian family every Sunday. We come together for that moment to see the truth of time in bread and wine, to see Christ uncovered in common things, among common people, that we may know how precious our time is. We recognize him uncovered in the Holy Meal that we may recognize him uncovered in every meal in every place among all people; that we may know that eternity comes into this moment. And eternity comes for this reason: the cross, which is eternal God crossing time-bound man and giving him His life.

So there is eternity. We know that. For that reason we can afford to struggle with small things. I can spend my time, hours of my time, struggling with the Community Renewal people as we pour over statistical tables about family income, and size, and age, and the ratio between income and rent. And know that I have wasted no time. Because *now* I am asking for better housing for my neighbors, for my parish. I am asking for it as loud and clear as I can. So I know my time is well spent. I do not know whether we will get it, or get it the way I think it should be. But I have given myself to asking.

Still there are so many moments I will never understand, moments whose connection I cannot understand; but in eternity they have a meaning. They are connected in patterns of inexplicable beauty into a resurrection which happened long ago and is the second coming and the end. In Christ the future and the present were long ago fulfilled.

Of course this is strange. No one ever said that Christians thought in simple-minded terms. Christians know that for God a thousand years are but as a day, and that every human *now* is already God's past. We know that even the future is past for God, that our lives are already played out and ended, and that *now* we already stand before the throne of God to face the judgment that has been amaking all these years.

Eternity means that though we live in isolated moments, each is desperately important. Life is no chess game in which shrewd men calculate their moves far into the future: if I move this way, he will move another, which means that I can move—and so on. Life is not like that. I do not understand the implications of my actions into the future. I do not know how they will affect another *now* yet to come.

There is, then, no action but the action *now* in best faith, in purest love, in fullest commitment, knowing that God controls eternity, that God alone gives to time pattern, significance, meaning, purpose, and direction. Perhaps the greatest sacrifice a Christian makes is to give up the search for meaning, to lay aside cares for the future in trust that a committed present prepares a future, worthy for a man to face.

There is, then, an urgency, a deep and compelling urgency about every action, because only independent actions create meaning and pattern.

So time acts, not death alone. This is the urgency. Time has no repetitions for me, and a moment lost is forever lost. And a seed perhaps has not been planted. It will be too late to plant the seed another day, because perhaps the seeds of another day will be different seeds, and the tree will grow alone and forsaken, an unneeded tree—as if now in the heart of New York I stood firm for the right of every man to till the soil, to have his plot of the rich earth to call his own, when instead men are begging for rat-free apartments and jobs worthy of their dignity and capacity.

A boy I know did a little house painting last summer. But there was not enough work for him. Our economy cares little for the slender shoots which are youth, the men of the future. No one cared enough to give him honest work. So when the lady of the house gave him a little painting to do and left for the day, he punched holes in her ceiling that he might have more work to give his hands the feel and dignity of honest toil, his pocketbook the fullness of earned money.

Death will not cut me off forever from my future, but the moment unanswered, the time wasted, the opportunity to face the present, these will cut me off and deny me another moment to face in the future.

So I live in many moments, all *now* for me. In this *now*, I write with six children dead in Birmingham, but you, dear reader, will read what I say in another moment, a moment with its own cares and distresses, a moment also to be answered. A moment which is present for us both.

The issues of today will not be answered with the replies of yesterday. You may look back and say some men were extreme in their single-minded attention to civil rights one hot summer; that they overlooked other issues equally pressing. Indeed they did, but they felt their moment demanded this single-mindedness. Another moment demands yet another mind.

The demands of *now* will always be one-sided and extreme because life is one-sided and extreme. The life of grace does not allow for law or clear definitions, does not allow for consistencies of method or approach, does not even allow for consistencies of institutions. Only spirit filled institutions survive, as do only spirit filled men who can shake off the dead hand of past issues and face the hot wind of new controversy.

The moment you and I face now is a moment made unique and precious because the cross has made every moment so. Often the moment is urgent, demanding action—action among people because their lives are so short, because their moments fly by; because the child beaten by his teacher last summer and all the others are older children now, moulded by what we have built around them, or dulled and pained by the horrors we have perpetrated by inaction and blindness to their needs.

I see every moment now in my mind's eye as I see the Holy Meal, precious, containing within it the fullness of death and resurrection: death, in that I must give up my self-mastery, my self-direction. I must give up the safety of treasured assumptions and superficial glances. I can no longer look at men as the world looks at them—trivial, persons of process and development, some lost, some saved by men's calculations. But I must now see them as God sees them—uncovered, their souls bared as my soul is bared, their hearts breaking and their souls enlarging at the miseries and the grandeurs of life. And all this to do *now*, not then.

The Holy Moment says that all creation must be viewed as the arena of God's action *now*. Firmly planted in the soil and in the hearts of men He offers life *now*. And in my mind's eye I hold a vision of a great round globe which is our world, and over it, towering, the figure of Christ challenging, pleading, weeping, smiling, telling me and all men to live and fulfill this globe and all other globes in all the universe into the fullness of His body. He is telling me to do it *now*—to waste not one second more.

But I know, too, that all this is only a picture of the mind, and that I will only see His purpose, only see His demand on me by looking into the eyes of my neighbor, by looking time in the face and responding in extreme action, in single-minded devotion, fully committed to the present, ready to be equally committed to future present moments whatever they demand, because it is my Lord who calls.

26. Communication

MALCOLM BOYD

It is an unmistakable irony that when many Christians worship Christ as the Lord of religion they deny Christ as the Lord of life.

Christ is placed in an eleven o'clock Sunday morning world (to reign as Lord for one hour a week), a news-magazine world ("religion" is a section of fragmented life along with "politics," "books" and "business"), a church-page world (Saturday is church-page day; "religion" is placed on a page, indeed, relegated to it). So when Christ is relegated to a position labeled "Lord of religion," He is taken out of a dynamic involvement in politics, sexuality, business, sociology, race, economics, and the arts; He is simply the Lord of religion.

Therefore, under such conditions, Christian communication takes place within a ghetto situation unrelated to the totality of human life. What is authentic communication? "I myself am afraid of the word 'communicate,' " W. D. Snodgrass, the Pulitzer Prize-winning poet, told a group of American college students. "In a sense, no poetry communicates at all," he said.

Communication is a word we frequently use indiscriminately and unthinkingly. There is a world of difference between the words "communication," and "communications."

Communications, from media to techniques and gimmicks,

fail all the time to bring about communication between one person and another person at a deep level of experience and concern. Most communications activity aimed at exploitation—resulting in a purchase or a vote or a conversion—does not want and cannot bear to find itself caught up in involvement, existential concern, or reality. Such a situation is, in fact, a judgment upon all forms of exploitation. Yet there is no communication possessing valid meaning which is lacking in involvement, existential concern, or reality.

This dilemma is a kind of backdrop for the whole drama of our contemporary struggle to achieve communication, particularly of the Christian Gospel.

It is self-contradictory for the Church to pronounce the Gospel message to men by means of communications if, by the very process, the individual listener, viewer, or reader is thereby reduced to the status of an object, statistic, or digit, and finds his personhood in peril. The Church dare not become yet another agent of dehumanization in a culture which daily tends to decrease the meaning of humanity and what it means to be a person. Can one save a statistic? If so, how? Can one love a statistic, especially if one's motivations are geared to exploitation instead of evangelism? If so, how?

In our communications complex, which often resembles the city of Enoch or a jungle of patchwork mazes, contemporary man needs and often wants and yearns for the hard questions. Are these questions being articulated by the churches and then given the answers found in the Gospel of Christ? Is Jesus Christ and the assurance of man's salvation in Him, being proclaimed by our so-called institutional Christian communications? Or, instead, is there simply the ultimate technicolored success story, absolutely fantastic and loaded with every element of drama one could ask for?

Christmas: BUY, BUY, BUY; hard-sell and gimmicks for Jesus; so-and-so shopping days until Xmas; Jesus Sells. Lent: dark, rainy, dreary days (but with gooey, buttered hot-cross

buns). And, then, Easter: candy, yellow sunny, and we're all in
the lonely big parade dancing in front of sugared crosses on Fifth
Avenue with Fred Astaire and Judy Garland.

The lonely big parade guarantees immunity from communication. "I like large parties. They're so intimate. At small parties
there isn't any privacy," commented Jordan Baker in F. Scott
Fitzgerald's *The Great Gatsby*. In the lonely big parade there is
the illusion of communication without the reality of communication.

So much that has been falsely labeled "Christian communications" is neither Christian nor communication.

Mistaken, false Christian communications has resulted in a
portrait of Christianity as sentimental, unrelated to the whole
of human life, a "proper" or "nice" pseudo-faith designed for
pragmatic self-improvement, and safely preserved, as a laboratory
specimen in alcohol, in a convenient, non-threatening class or
race structure.

One of the most tragic and savage gulfs existing in the Church
at the present time has occurred because men, angrily, and with
considerable passion, have come to define the meanings of "religion," "religious" and "Christian" quite differently.

Some churchmen honestly define religion as something taking
place within the church sanctuary, period; others define religion
as something taking place in God's whole creation including the
church sanctuary. Some define a religious play or other work of
art as one concerning a specific religious or biblical subject, as,
for example, the Hollywood biblical movies; others define a religious play or other work of art as one concerning man living
in the hand of the living God, whether or not man is aware there
is a God.

There is explicit and implicit Christian witness and communication. It must be said that witness is another word which
can have vastly different meanings for different persons. Does
one make a witness about something mechanically, starting here
and stopping there, as one might turn a water faucet on and off?
Is witness self-conscious, deliberate, stylized, even possessed of

the meaning of its own righteousness; or is it, on the other hand, unself-conscious, nonchalant, free, a Spirit-filled action which is the work and doing of God rather than of man?

Explicit Christian communication may be found in a stylized sense in the Christian sermon. Implicit Christian communication recognizes the partial bankruptcy of all our verbalisms and, too, the fact that the proclamation of the Gospel is not limited to any form; that the preachment of the Word of God is not limited to a structured, verbal presentation within a liturgical mold. In fact, as the liturgy itself must be integrally related to life in order to contain within itself the depth and profundity of inner and spiritual grace enlivening outward and visible sign, so must the proclamation of the Word of God be Spirit-motivated and filled, channeling and liberating inward and spiritual grace in outward and visible sign.

Much implicit Christian communication is an overlapping of explicit Christian communication, undergirding or transcending it, interpreting it, translating it into cultural idiom and image. For example, much art which is not at all explicitly religious or Christian is, in striking ways, implicitly Christian. Such art has been called "negative witness," giving a Christian picture of hell by telling about life without God or self-giving, without love or abandonment. Such art may depict man's pride, self-loving, and self-pity, indeed his attempt to make sense of his universe and life without God or self-giving, without love or abandonment.

This kind of art shows how life is then brutal, even in acts of brittle outward kindnesses which are not kind; how life is then arid, mere existence, the round perpetuating itself and feeding on time, a very horror even in the subtly crude disguises of pleasantries without joy. Such portrayal can be a most telling, implicit kind of Christian communication: *this* (it says) is the charade, the desert, the abyss, the existing death which is not death, the automation, the predicament and situation in which one says, "I do not know who is God, or my brother, or myself."

Prostituted, would-be Christian communication which seeks

to disguise the human condition under stereotypes and carica-
tures of that condition is increasingly being refuted or laughed at.
This particular message more and more cries out that something
is phony, vacuous, lacking: "life isn't *like* that."

From barmaid to tough, competitive debutante, anyone over
ten years of age knows something stark and terribly real about
the nature of life. After all, this is the culture which knows that
the United States has atom-bombed Japan, millions of Jews
have been exterminated in vestigially Christian Germany, two
World Wars have been fought, racial strife has erupted from
South Africa to Alabama, and now the Bomb seems to hang,
like a hideous Damocles sword, over the whole of the earth.

Ours is the culture, too, which has looked hard and close into
the bitter face of prejudice, the beery-red face of nationalistic
jingoism, and even the empty smiling face of material plenty
covering up the jagged, bleeding wounds of spiritual rape.

How to communicate this? It cannot be a fundamentalistic,
literal communication: no one would believe it, no one could
stand it; immediately there would spring up rationalizations to
deny the truth, validity, and challenge of it. But it can be portrayed identifiably, poetically, existentially, unmistakably, in a
way surpassing and past rationalizations.

The artist, for one, can so communicate this message. When
I lived and worked in the Taizé community in France several
years ago I saw frère Eric's painting entitled simply "Explosion
Atomique." He was not dealing with literal atomic or nuclear
explosion but with our modern tower of Babel: the winding,
suddenly breaking-off pathways of our culture; the promontories
overlooking the abyss; the many avenues of seeming and could-be
dialogue ending in ditches and clouds and nothingness.

There is sound and fury in the sweet life. There are psychological fox-holes everywhere, and men are fighting other men and
themselves in undeclared and declared wars. The starched lace
curtains have been ripped off the front of nice bourgeois, yellow-
and-white, proper houses of the soul, revealing a filth identifiable

as self-righteousness and selfishness so shocking that it has already created layer upon layer of sheer guilt.

Interestingly, the theatre at its best, or its most promising, has unmasked reality where the pulpits have either not dared do it, or else have strangely lacked the spiritual resources for speaking prophetically.

Too, we have encountered prophetic speaking in contemporary dance, in reading of poetry and folk-singing, in such a musical composition as Menotti's *The Consul*. A number of films, primarily coming from Europe, England, and Asia, and seldom coming out of Hollywood, have torn away pretenses, revealing to us the face of that reality of the human condition which Jesus Christ came into the world, as God and as man, to redeem from lostness and meaninglessness.

Many persons have commented critically about the tastelessness of the amorality portrayed in a number of realistic contemporary films. Yet it is an amorality present in our culture, even to be found (though it will come as an uncomprehended shock) within our borgeois-oriented, properly-structured mass life of good intentions, honored traditions and erratically sick actions, which seem not to be related to anything other than themselves.

It is the human condition, even at its rawest, in its most extreme aberrations and perversions, in its sickness unto death, in its most self-loving affirmations of purposelessness, that Jesus Christ has come into the world to save. There is no estrangement between any evil or sickness of the twentieth century and the Gospel of Jesus Christ, despite all the evident estrangement between life, on the one hand, and churches, on the other.

Prostituted, would-be Christian communication has long ago publicly denied the existence of resurrection as well as of death; it has instead hazily connected the good life to an immortality which is a bland extension of life. However, Christian communication has a Gospel to proclaim—that resurrection comes after death, for Jesus Christ and for those who, having been baptized into His death, are recipients by grace of His gift to them of newness of life.

Christians experience a prefiguring of the meaning of death and resurrection in their own sharp deaths unto self, and the stirrings of renewal which come afterwards. This meaning has been expressed vividly in art.

In Grunewald's portrayal of the crucifixion of Christ in the Issenheim altarpiece, one comes face-to-face with the sheer death of the event of Golgotha. In Carol Reed's great film *Odd Man Out*, one shares the feelings of a man, hunted, alone, inexorably coming to his death because no one will love him enough—as a man, a human being, a child of God—to come to his help. In Tennessee Williams' play *Camino Real*, one shares the feeling of death and hell hanging over the life-scene on the stage, then is braced and startled to hear the redemptive speech: "In a place where so many are lonely, it would be inexcusably selfish to be lonely alone."

What does salvation mean, quite specifically and quite personally, in our dehumanized, urban, technical culture, marked by loneliness in crowds, and within the fierce pain in one's own personality? Surely salvation does not mean togetherness: with what a hard laugh man has obliterated the cruel fancy of that organization word. But it does mean relatedness, involvement, concern, sharing, feeling, belonging, accepting and being accepted for oneself.

Perhaps we have out-communicated ourselves. We have said too much, or so very much, or at least everything that could almost conceivably be said about a number of vital, pressing problems. We have talked and talked and talked, and not acted. We have written and written and written, and not acted. Possibly, then, our most communicable communication is simply that we indeed know what we should have done and have not done it.

What do we intend to do with the heavy burden of such paradoxical communication?

We have come full circle: our own words have caught up with us. When we speak about "love," someone can catch us up immediately by interjecting: "Ah! You speak of love again. You taught me so well what the word means, and what dreadful strength the image holds, that I perceive now only your own failure to manifest love. Are you still saying and teaching the same things about love, or, in line with your evident actions, have you altered your ideas about it?"

Feelings communicate forcefully, with or without politely respectable smiles and diplomatic remarks; so do images mirroring real situations, motivations, and attitudes themselves. Love as a concept, or even a word, must be redeemed, baptized in a great ceremony which will see the washing away of its foolish semanticisms and cruel images. Love is not a word reserved for use either in bed or at church conventions; it must also be understood as social justice in action.

The Gospel is always in the process of communicating itself, that is, being communicated by the Holy Spirit of God. We are, therefore, agents of communication by personal intention and commitment, or else agents of communication without any clear idea as to what we are doing. For to be human, to be alive, is to be engaged in the process of communication; and every man is engaged in communication of the Gospel—communicating his explicit acceptance or rejection of it, his implicit acceptance or rejection of it; the reasons in his life and in his reactions toward his society which serve to dictate his attitudes toward it.

Nominal Christians set up roadblocks to meaningful communication of the Gospel, and often remain consciously unaware of such fifth-column activity within the life of the Church. For example, the Gospel calls men to humanness; any form of dehumanization, as manifested in any kind of race or class discrimination, contributes to setting up active opposition to the Gospel. The Gospel calls men to unity; the divided Church on earth, especially when there is an expression of human pride in separation, witnesses to the supremacy of the will of man over the will of God. The Gospel calls men to love of God and each other; human idolatries, especially of "churchianity" and things

pertaining to it, often represent blasphemies which are con-
veniently and outrageously cloaked in so-called religious imagery
and humanly sinful self-righteousness.

When we worship Christ as the Lord of religion, and of religion alone, we are communicating more forcefully than we
can know that Christ is not the Lord of the whole of life. When,
by our attitudes and actions, we do not honor and obey Christ
as the Lord of politics, economics, sociology, indeed, as the Lord
of the totality of human life *including religion,* we announce
publicly and resoundingly that Christ is irrelevant to the profound questions which stir and control men's lives.

PART IV

———————————

EPILOGUE

27. Prayer and Social Issues

DOM BENEDICT REID, O.S.B.

God is passionately in love with man. He made this beautiful human animal with a mind and heart to know and love all that exists, and lifted him up to return the divine passion. In the exuberance of His love, God made man free, giving him a supreme share in the divine image and likeness.

The excitement of the free possession of his magnificent nature moved man to turn away from the divine lover. By this rejection man created the essential social issue, groups of men in conflict with themselves, with other men, and with their God. Yet the very conflict is a dynamic movement, a restless search. The word "issue" means just this, a passing through. Man's social issues boil out of his vigorous and even violent passing through the world in his search for the truth and goodness that alone can fulfill his nature.

How can God honor His creature's true freedom and still give him the infinite truth and goodness that alone will satisfy him? How does anyone pursue a rebellious child? You go ahead of him and touch him in his deepest self. From *within* the conflicts of human social issues, God searches the heart and mind of man, sounding the call of a Father. When man hears this call, he knows himself to be a son or daughter (II Cor. 6:18), and thereby knows the human race as brothers and sisters in the Father's family. God's brooding prayer-call invites man to the

251

divine love which is the true fulfillment of his precarious passage through time: "I will be your God, and ye shall be my people" (Jer. 7:23).

In whatever way the love of God is presented, we must admit that most of the contemporary world does not understand or believe. Is it unfair to say that even the churches do not understand or believe? That would be an insult to God and to millions of faithful Christians. But it may also be an insult, even blasphemy, to ignore the love of God for the greater number of millions who still long to find Him. Unless God is discerned at the heart of man's society, the social issues themselves infect and wound all who are involved. The thrust and counter-thrust of ambitious and frustrated men makes a boiling chaos of an ever shrinking world. Asian flu and unnatural hostility travel just as quickly, and infect as unfailingly. We must act thoughtfully, prayerfully, but without sloth, on behalf of believers and unbelievers. If God's love is in some degree understood and returned, then we are commissioned by the divine brooding to show it to others. If we ourselves are uncertain of God's love (and who can ever be complacent?), then we also are in restless search of Him who pursues us from within our nature—just outside our pride. It is love, as the Commandments say, that is at issue, God's love and man's love.

God takes the initiative in this love affair. He prays for us and in us. Christ who is God puts this prayer *into* us, "Our Father"; and the Spirit who is God, knowing that we don't know how to pray, intercedes for us "with groanings which cannot be uttered" (Rom. 8:26). It is a half-true instinct, then, that guides pressure groups to raise up a father figure. God puts this prayer deep in our nature. The groanings, too, of underprivileged minorities are an intercession wrung from the human heart by a divine compassion. God prays first. Our prayer is a response.

God's prayer comes from His very being. He exists in absolute independence and absolute perfection. He is infinite goodness, truth, and beauty who neither needs to receive from, or give to, anything outside Himself. Looking at the absolute nature of God in the stark shorthand of theology (which is only what God has told us about Himself), we are stunned in mind and heart. God is so far away. Yet we have only to look candidly within ourselves to find the vigorous structure, now twisted, of the image and likeness of Him who made us. Our pride is a sin-sick view of our being, destined as that being is to share in the divine independence and perfection. No human pressure group can ever successfully promote man's true being. The God of our being is our best lobby power, sustaining every prayer of the heart and every reach of the mind.

God is utterly unique in His being, but He is not solitary—He is a family. The divine nature is possessed by three Persons. Here in God's being is the essence of prayer and love: the Father and His Son and their Love live an infinite sharing of goodness and truth. Each Person loves His divine neighbor as He loves Himself, which is perfect individuality and perfect unity—the perfect pattern of a family and a society. So how does God's social life help us with our battle over, say, civil rights? Does a man have rights because the state or the economy gives them to him? No. A man's rights come from his God-given nature and his membership in God's family. If the state or the economy does not recognize these rights, men may have to claim them. One Southern integration leader summoned his people to prayer and penance as a necessary purification before demonstration. Whoever prays will find God's will in the social issue.

Man is a family animal. He struggles desperately to belong. The tragedy in social issues is that man does not know the full implication of this desire. We were created to belong to God's family by being made partakers of the divine nature itself (II Pet. 1:4). This is indeed a magnificent promise, but if I do not feel I belong in my own human family, how can I believe this incredible promise? Some terrible curse frustrates my family life. I withdraw into myself, and freely remain there—in great loneliness. My selfishness and my freedom bar me from belonging, and I pretend to prefer this separation because I will not surrender *myself*. In our separation from our common father we

inevitably quarrel violently among ourselves, and in the quarreling lose our true dignity and our belonging to one another. Fallen
man's society is the reverse image of God's family and wrings out
of us our most agonizing prayer, "Have mercy." Even our blasphemies and curses are tortured prayers. The human issue is to
pass through life in dignity and love, and we cannot do that
without God. "Damn," goes up the prayer.

God listens to every prayer and answers it with His love:
"Before they call, I will answer; and while they are yet speaking,
I will hear" (Isa. 65:24). In the fullness of His prayer-answer,
He sent His Son to make His prayer audible, substantial. Christ
is the Father's prayer made flesh. Since the Incarnation, man has
an Older Brother to pass through life with him. The issue has
been clarified. God lives and prays *among* us in His Son, and all
who belong to the Son are members of His Body the Church
(Col. 1:24). The Church's prayer, then, is Christ's prayer, whether
turned to the Father in adoration or to the wandering children
in longing invitation and instruction. Why doesn't the world see
Christ in the Church praying? We can read the answer in His
eyes—if we dare to look into them in the poor, the sick, the
rejected.

From the point of view of this book, which is a desperate appeal for Christian renewal, the first involvement of the Church
is with her Head, Jesus Christ, for He is life. Out of Him pours
forth the dynamic source of all contemporary life: "In him was
life; and the life was the light of men" (John 1:4). He owns all
life and therefore claims each wound of society as His own:
"Inasmuch as ye have done it unto one of the least of these my
brethren, ye have done it unto me" (Matt. 25:40). Prayer
plunges us into life, into Christ, and through Him into every
social issue in the world—right up to the Cross.

The Christian who prays in Christ suffers, for the Cross attracts
evil; nor is he able to say to the mountain causing the burden,
"remove hence." Rather through prayer he discovers the risen
Christ reigning victoriously *within* every personal and corporate
wound of man. Christ is our passover by entering into each

human and social issue to carry through those who can bear
His love. His love is a terrible glory, a whirlwind of justice which
the Old Testament prophets manifested in frightening splendor.
The fury of a race riot is a modern prophecy, showing us that
"Christ came not to send peace, but a sword" (Matt. 10:34).
Prayer takes us straight to that Love at the center of the social
warfare.

So far we have not discussed prayer in the usual terms. We
have looked at its essential identification with the being and
action of God, and with the nature of man, Being to being,
Nature to nature, Deep to deep, Life to life. Any other foundation for prayer leads to sentimentality and superficiality, the two
most damning accusations of prayer made by the world. What is
rightly so judged is not the prayer of God, but the musings (no
matter how beautiful) of man.

We come then to the issue of our humanness. We have already noted the magnificence of man's nature, made to know
and love, ultimately, God Himself. We have seen the appalling
cost of rejecting God and thereby losing control of the human
nature. Man is a great lover, at war with himself. Our true freedom suggests to some that prayer is unnecessary, while our pro-
foundly disordered nature—"what I hate, that do I" (Rom. 7:15)
—convinces others that it is unavailing. But neither freedom nor
disorder can change man's dependent nature, which is the result
of God's love, and the rational basis for an ordered rule of prayer.
The work of prayer not only puts us *in* Christ, but puts us also
squarely in the middle of our own human condition. Is this not
proof that prayer is real?

By baptism, Christ unites our humanness to Himself that He
may live His life, death, and resurrection in us. He strengthens
this union through the Sacraments, that our life and prayer may
increasingly become the living, breathing, sweating action of the
Body of Christ. His prayer finally wells up *within* our own being,
"Father, . . . that they may be one, as we are" (John 17:11).
One Christian surrounded by a Black Muslim group was forced
into the very substance of his baptismal union with Christ while

their spokesman poured hate and ridicule into him. He took it, and prayed. In the end the spokesman broke down and cried.

We Christians do not ordinarily live at the core of our baptism: "Watch out for me today, Lord, or I may betray you," said one of the saints. If we lived our baptism, we would be quite clear about the world, the flesh, and the devil. Death and Christian discipline (asceticism) would have a positive place in our affirmation of God. The social issues would move more quickly and directly toward their appointed purpose in God's plan.

The central action of the living Christ is His sacrificial worship of the Father. When we trace out the implications of these words—"central action" includes His present reign in heaven and all His earthly mysteries, "the living Christ" embraces all who have been or will be baptised, "sacrificial worship" means the offering up of His human nature and thereby all of creation, "the Father" signifies the God who made us and to whom we are to return—we realize that Christ is our liturgy. He is our passover, the One who carries our human issues through to the Father. *Within* the liturgical passover celebration, Christ feeds the people of God with His own Body and Blood that we may pass daily from death to life, from sin to charity, and ultimately from earth to eternity. This atoning, redeeming, glorifying worship is liturgy, enacted daily in quiet simplicity or splendid grandeur in the churches throughout the world. Clearly, we must bring social issues, the racial issue for example, into the Eucharist. Perhaps on occasion we invite an outsider to pray it with us. If we cannot communicate sacramentally with them, then we bear that pain as an intercession.

Parish life should be a preparation for, and an extension of, the Eucharist. The people of God in gathering around the altar to celebrate the passover of God come closer to each other, learning to supply the little ordinary human needs of folk on a journey through the world. Parish life is therefore a dialogue of charity between God and man, and man and man. This is the first mission for the priest and the people, the beginning of Church unity. From this parish charity we go out in humility and openness to others. To listen and to serve with a Eucharistically strengthened heart and mind is really what separated Christians and unchurched people need most from one another. This charity, deepened and extended, will in God's own way and time lead us to Him in the issue of over-all unity. It is also the exchange of charity among the members of the parish that is the most effective sign to the neighborhood that Christ is passing through their midst. The parish is a priest for the neighborhood. Almost any good work—education, race harmony, liturgy and arts, family counselling, etc.—can reach out effectively from the parish family if it is grounded in Eucharistic charity. This is the parish rule of prayer which should be given first place when the individual makes up his personal rule. It is better to pray and act with the parish than to develop a separated spirituality, no matter how intense and satisfying. Even highly gifted contemplates are not isolationists.

Ideally, the family will be established in the parish, gathering around its altar and sharing its life of charity. But then the broken home is more nearly the issue today. Suppose father is an alcoholic. Then we must pray to Christ *within* that person. Above all we must respect the human person, so alienated even from himself. "I was a stranger, and ye took me in" (Matt. 25:35). Probably we can at least manage grace at table, which significantly relates the family meal to the parish Eucharistic meal. Such a simple prayer reveals Christ already present in the home and opens up the possibility of family conversion. When the family discovers the Lord *within* family issues, there is an experience of joy, of coming together in Love.

If we merely endure one another in surface politeness or barely concealed resentment, there is another god in charge. Family prayer establishes the true God. The parish priest will gladly instruct the family in saying the Prayer Book Offices. Perhaps one Office a week would be enough to begin a revolution in the home. The Gospel for the week is an illuminating interpretation on the day's activities of each member. A Bible Commentary with a dictionary and an atlas are the beginning tools to make of the evening meal a delightful educational adventure, with father and mother as the first guides in the wisdom of living. From such prayer and education, young people can gain the judgment to make the choices required of them in the contemporary world, where their entertainment and independence can suddenly expose them to raw evil when they may be least prepared. The family issues of marriage fidelity, economy, entertainment, manners, education, arts and crafts, relating as they do to the parish and neighborhood life, are all small editions of the issues of the whole world. The home is the first school for living, and prayer is the key to living in Christ there, and everywhere.

With the parish Eucharist and the family as the basic context, we can look at the elements of a rule of life which will include the Eucharist and some part of the Offices of the Church, observance of fasting and abstinence, grace at meals, a disciplined consecration of a portion of one's income for God's work, and Scripture study. The more these elements of a rule can be practiced in the parish or the home, the more visible Christ will be in and through my life. Private prayers (so-called), such as meditation and devotions, are still acts of the whole Christ. Even our distractions in prayer may be a call to be more charitably involved in some specific issue. But prayer and action are one in Christ and cannot, therefore, be in opposition to one another. Those who give up prayer because action is so desperately needed may be imposing one more issue on the already chaotic issue, egoism.

"The effectual fervent prayer of a righteous man availeth much" (James 5:16). One may go to India, or jail, or to confession. So long as we go in Christ we pray and act with redeeming power. Christ has already redeemed the world. The Christian is to show the world that its redeemer lives *within* the very social issues themselves. If local politics are inefficient or corrupt, I should at least inform myself of the issues of justice involved. A few informed neighbors, educating others, have in specific instances prevented a big political machine from an unwise urban renewal push. Or take race—wouldn't you be encouraged (whatever your color) to see a person wearing a button, all black with a white equal-sign? What about socially unacceptable people, like epileptics? Would you invite one to your home for an evening? World peace begins with the Prince of Peace, employing His principles at home and at work. Send a small gift and a prayer to a priest in a distressed area of the world, and you lift up the hands that lift up the world to God.

There are a hundred more social issues—nuclear weapons, the United Nations, technology and man, common understanding of natural law, the ethics of communications, passive resistance and active intervention—all these trouble our world and our selfish complacency. Christ has His reasons for allowing the devil jurisdiction in the world, but Christ is present too. He waits dynamically and acts invitingly *within* the world, summoning the members of His Body to pray and act with Him ". . . that God in all things may be glorified through Jesus Christ, to whom be praise and dominion for ever and ever. Amen" (I Pet. 4:11).